OUR MOTHERS

" DISILLUSIONED : From a problem picture by T. B. Kennington in the Royal Academy " (1894)

OUR MOTHERS

EDITED BY
ALAN BOTT

TEXT BY
IRENE CLEPHANE

A Cavalcade in Pictures, Quotation
and Description of Late
Victorian Women
1870–1900

BENJAMIN BLOM   New York/London

" THE OLD LOVE AND THE NEW : The morning bicycle parade, Hyde Park " (1896)

TO
P.H.C.

CONTENTS

		PAGE
" GIRL OF THE PERIOD ": A PREFACE		2
I.	SOMEBODIES AND NOBODIES	11
II.	" THE ENGLISH LIVE AT HOME "	51
III.	DOWN AMONG THE MASSES	79
IV.	INTO THE OPEN	105
V.	TOWARDS EMANCIPATION	137
VI.	GOOD WORKS AND SWEET CHARITY	170
VII.	" STEEL-BOUND AND WHALEBONE-LINED "	191

First Published 1932
Reissued 1969 by
Benjamin Blom, Inc. Bronx, New York 10452
and 56 Doughty Street, London, W.C. I

Library of Congress Catalog Card Number 73-81513

93693

Printed in the United States of America

"GIRL OF THE PERIOD" : A PREFACE

VICTORIANISM, as a word, has become more blessed than Mesopotamia ; and it is just as vague. Invited to describe her idea of the young person in the eighteen-seventies, a young person of nowadays would use much the same language as she would use for a girl of the eighteen-fifties. Bustles might alternate with crinolines in the description, but from either era there would be conjured up a fragrant, simpering, obedient, home-bound piece of human bric-à-brac. Miasma still covers, in popular eyes, the varied procession of Victorian life, in despite of books that praise, ridicule or analyse the Great Victorians. An amusing light opera about Victorians came to London this year by way of undergraduate Cambridge. Its period was the Crimean War ; but I noted in its dress and dialogue items that derived from five different decades.

Our phase is late Victorian, from about 1870 to the end of the century. I attend here, by way of preface, to the girl of the period, because she alone seems to have been left on the mat by Miss Irene Clephane, who has written introductions to the chapters of illustration. Our narrative is mostly told through woodcuts by nineteenth-century engravers ; and my part has been restricted to editing the record and adapting the pictures, with their contemporary quotations. I wrote too dogmatically in *Our Fathers* ; and when a companion volume on *Our Mothers* was invited, it seemed right that a woman should contribute the text, and that she should be my collaborator who had sifted hundreds of thousands of engravings to find the three hundred in *Our Fathers*. She has given so much patience and understanding to her research that in 1870 there is left to myself only a girl with rump and bosom stuffed by queer protrusions, but with a sparkling challenge in her eyes.

This girl, in outlook and appearance, denies the solid, mid-Victorian era that has almost gone. Demureness and excessive propriety, after their long innings, have lost favour. It is one of those recurring moments in the history of manners when young women of means, declining to be bored, determine to shock. Prudery diminishes in the 'seventies, blushes are trained to appear less often, the code for flirtation relaxes. The denouncer's cry is loud in the land ; his hands are upraised because the girl of the period is fast. Pleasure is said to be her occupation, marriage into luxury her single ambition. Also, she tints her face with paint that denies nature and is therefore deceitful to men. The leading comic journal attacks her pert tongue and her slang.

Aria da capo. For a parallel to the denunciation one need not move forward to Dean Inge. I quote from a letter to *The Ladies' Magazine* of 1800, seven decades earlier : " Young women of to-day live in a perpetual round of amusement. They go about in perfect freedom. Their sole occupation is to walk, and drive, and amuse themselves with dancing. They read the most improper books, and the foam of a poisonous philosophy falls from their lips."

Most of that quotation (which might be a paraphrase from the dirge sung by praisers of bygone times in the Press of the early nineteen-twenties) was echoed in the 'seventies. Admittedly, their girl of the period did not go about in perfect freedom ; but the rest of the 1800 indictment again applied before 1880. Garden parties, river parties, picnics, balls, dinners, tea-tattles, informal routs, musicales, bazaars, archery, croquet and the new lawn tennis belonged to her " perpetual round of amusement." As for improper books, she was an apt smuggler into the bedroom drawer of those sensual *Poems and Ballads*, by Algernon Swinburne (a young aristocrat dubbed " swineborn " by the comic journal already mentioned, because of his lascivious writings). And if no foam of poisonous philosophy fell from her lips (she had been too frivolous to take sides in the Darwinian conflict as to whether her early ancestors were apes or angels) her inclination was to back impudent new upstarts like Mr. Whistler against fine old panjandrums like Mr. Ruskin.

None of this tallies with to-day's popular conception of a Victorian girl of the world. Nor, on the other side of the critical picture, does this from *The Graphic* in the late 'seventies : " For the fashionable beauty, life is an endless carnival, and dress a round of disguises. She does everything, and the wings of Mercury might be attached to her tiny *bottines*, so rapid are her changes of scene and character. She is a sportswoman, an athlete, a ballroom divinity. She is alternately a horsewoman, a huntress, a bold and skilful swimmer ; she drives a pair of horses like a charioteer, mounts the roof of a four-in-hand, plays lawn tennis, is at home on a racecourse or the deck of a fast yacht. She is a judge of the refinements of dining and has a pretty taste in vintages. She is a power at the theatre or the opera ; and none is more brilliant at a supper party. Of the modern young lady à la mode, who wields alike the fiddle bow, the billiard cue and the etching needle, who climbs mountains and knows the gymnasium, none but herself can be the prototype."

Allowing for exaggeration in the detail, enough remains to show that this Queen of the May was not a fragility shielded always, like her forerunner, from the wind of immodesty. Nor was she terribly modest in conversation. The facts of sex were not openly discussed, but they made the disguised running in her contacts with men. Opulent womanliness was her attitude, which countered the excessive manliness of the type represented by Ouida's heroes, then at their extreme in best-selling absurdity. At the dinner table as at the garden party, the female partner's line was arch banter, and the male partner's was thrusting flattery ; but the fundamental theme, invisible beneath thick petticoats of hidden meaning, was sex-attraction. Social success often depended upon the girl's talent for badinage. She was complimented, rather than affronted, by attacks on her flightiness. She had before her the thrilling example of the Marlborough House Set, clustering round Royal Highnesses of Wales, whose lively doings (by contrast with stodgy correctitude in the Queen's circle) she applauded when critical Puritans gave tongue. And when, late in the 'seventies, Mrs. Langtry, actress-daughter of a divine and friend of the Prince, sprang into the centre of

London's limelight, and was made welcome in noble houses, here again was an exciting model for her brief hour of modernity.

Dress had adapted itself, as always, to the changing manners. The fashions did not admit to a concentration on sex, but this was their evident effect, through emphasis on female particularities. The crinoline had been secretive and, despite its girth, delicate. The bustle was neither : it was an artificial enlargement of the posterior curve. (It also had other uses—I know an elderly, much-moustached poet whose mother's discarded bustles were habitually adapted for riding-a-cock-horse in the nursery.) It was balanced in front by an artificial enlargement of the curve of the bust, caused by tight lacing beneath, and helped when necessary by a padding. Contrast invited attention to flanks, loins and the expanses below the bust : satin or other material was stretched over them with violent tightness. And, woman's other glory being her hair, this was used for a crowning extension at the back, with artificial swathes, fringes and pin-curls to increase its seeming bulk. The modes of the 'seventies were not graceful, but they managed to proclaim rich bargains in flesh beneath the copious packing. A census in the 'seventies showed that the proportion of marriages had risen by twelve per thousand of population.

What, then, remained of the mid-Victorian rigidities, which twentieth-century legend has fastened upon all Victorian women before the 'nineties ? The process of changing social attitudes was gradual. The girl of the 'seventies kept to fundamental taboos. Her business was to marry well, but union at the altar must be regarded as unbreakable, whatever the unhappiness it brought ; and the existence of an amoral half-world for men only, which was outside her radius, could not be recognised. She must not travel alone, whether by cab or railway. Nor, without chaperon, could she go to ball, theatre or any public entertainment (the unexacting chaperon, however, could serve for a dozen couples at a river party ; and in the ballroom she seldom enforced for every dance the return of her charges, who in any case were glad of the excuse to return when partners failed to stimulate). Finally, the vaunted part in athletics of the girl of the 'seventies seldom went beyond playing at the playing of games. It was kept subordinate to the needs of sex-specialisation ; it imposed nothing in the way of relief from padding, toe-tripping from long skirts, and frantic corsetings. The seventeen-inch waist was never relaxed except in the privacy of home. Exercise, like hygiene and health itself, meant little to the late Victorian figure. The freedom of the limbs was neither won nor sought, except by a few cranks for " rational dress." Feminine tennis, in particular, was a pleasant absurdity when it arrived during the 'seventies.

The next girl of the period, in the eighteen-eighties, went further in athletics, as in emancipation and frivolity ; and she produced champions of all three. There was no alliance between the fashionable young person and the earnest " new woman," but up to a point each travelled in the same direction. Both wanted liberties, and the advance of either spurred on the other. A difference was that whereas the " new woman " had to brave ridicule for her aims in education or suffrage, the girl à la mode, emulating Marlborough House, not only took indulgences in her stride, but made them the fashion. In the 'eighties, moreover, Matthew Arnold's fling at the upper classes, that they were the barbarians of culture, still hit home, except in the case of scholars and selective Souls ; and the female of the species showed less regard than the male for education. She reflected the mid-Victorian young woman who explained her ignorance of history by saying, " To tell the truth, Uncle, I don't care a bit what anybody ever did." She, as a majority, was benevolently amused by the small minority's striving after girls' colleges, women's votes and degrees for women doctors. She approved the struggle, but from a distance. Instinct told her that desire for education was not its only cause, a more urgent one being the shortage of husbands. Frontier wars and Empire building took shoals of young men abroad, but the young women went no farther than to Paris for finishing school. The mass mind associated the eternal " superfluous woman " with female graduates, as well as with downtrodden governesses. And since marriage was beyond even pleasure as an urge for the girl of the period, all hail to emancipated vestals that awed the male barbarian, and so removed themselves from competition.

Little remained by now of the mid-Victorian poses, as formerly worn by young ladies. The girl of the later 'eighties had assurance, she was strenuous in games, flaunted her attitudes as clearly as she flaunted her padded shape. She took up crazes, whether for coaching, slumming or the new teashops. She flattered with imitation American heiresses who, like the millionaires from South Africa, were forcing the doors of " Society." She was definitely more Mary than Martha. She was apt to patronise her father (the heavy Pater-familias had declined with mutton-chop whiskers). Far, far away was the un-happy land where she would have had to pretend vapours and an innocence so extreme as to be indecent.

She was luckier than her elder sister from the 'seventies, now married. Matrons in the 'eighties had their Married Women's Property Act, but less opportunity than the vivacious maidens for avoiding the pale, standardised gentility that clutched at all middle-class homes. But by the time when the girl from the 'eighties had married into the 'nineties, custom permitted young mares to be as skittish as the fillies. It was in this deafening, gimcrack, rip-roaring decade of display and easy wealth that the term " girl " was extended for application to matrons in their early twenties. In London (it is always the type in the capital city, and of comfortable background, whom the future picks as girl-of-the-period) the girls, married and unmarried, made fin-de-siècle a favourite adjective, and took it to mean flaunted change. They kicked over a dozen lingering traces, beginning with the bustle. Self-confidence taught them to rely on the female form as only God and the corset manufacturer had made it. Above the middle, they exposed across the dinner table vast sections of fine English breast (Victorian decency's dread of the bared form was one of the things discarded). They reddened their lips like Medusa's, and provoked Mr. Beerbohm into essays on their pervasion of rouge. They insisted on being " different," and used Dolly-dialogue flippancy to deny the past. They adventured over thin ice for conversational skating between the sexes. They openly discussed the ethics and incidents of divorce cases, in the courts or the Pinero drama (it was in the 'nineties that women who divorced their husbands began to be " received " everywhere except at Court). They brought bravado to their open yearning over George Alexander and the matinée idols. They rushed in droves upon the safety bicycle. They became so vigorous that the Press printed complaints of their excessive exercise. They took to fencing, to the American Barn Dance (the prologue to ballroom jazz), to *The Daily Mail's* bright new journalism, and to jaunting, without regard for jeers, in the early motor-cars so soon as the red-flag restriction went. Some of them took to smoking in the home or the college study. They gushed, but they were anything except Victorian.

The 'nineties were a rich, remarkable period for women of the classes (down among the masses, as a later chapter shows, the female was so browbeaten by her conditions that she had time only for breeding and keeping alive). It is probable that they ruled the social roost more definitely, though in another manner, than our own women have done. Plumed hens o' the North made the manners, the fads, the slang, much of the scandal, half the epigrams and all the social running. They did more than insist on having minds of their own ; they made self-will as fashionable as the Gibson Girl's regality. All ages took part in the feminine assertiveness. The ex-girl of the 'seventies returned into the picture as a domineering old lady with lorgnettes. The girl from the 'eighties had become " the woman of thirty," who was the latest fashion in heroines for playwrights and novelists. And the girl of the 'nineties, without knowing quite what she wanted, backed her own fancies against her parents'. A minority of her translated into real life Mr. Bernard Shaw's early, aggressive heroines, who demanded careers and self-propulsion. We leave her, at the century's end, still strangling her body with fantastic corsetry, but looking into a feminised future which she has largely helped to fashion.

ALAN BOTT

Grateful acknowledgement is due to the proprietors of The Graphic *who have permitted the selection of 167 illustrations from their files, and also to the proprietors of* The Queen *who have permitted the selection of 51 illustrations.*

" P. AND O. BELLE : On voyages to India the male sex predominates, and when only one young lady is aboard, she receives vast attention from susceptible males. One acts as her punkah-wallah, and the rest undertake any task she desires " (1877)

" HEAVEN'S ARTILLERY : Visitors to the ' Cage ' above the Monument on Whit-Monday were literally ' in the clouds.' The play of Heaven's high artillery was vastly impressive. The new cage prevents suicide, six persons having previously cast themselves down " (1874)

IN THE STALLS AT THE EMPIRE THEATRE (1894)

AFTER THE DRAWING ROOM : A VISIT TO THE PHOTOGRAPHER (1895)

" FOUR IN HAND : A coaching revival comes from the new Four-in-Hand Club, in St. James's Street, which has 60 teams and is a good customer to breeders. The members, if not all noblemen, are authentic sporting gentlemen. Young ladies are enthusiastic passengers " (1871)

OUR MOTHERS

I

SOMEBODIES AND NOBODIES

THOSE who have always moved in middle class circles do not write auto-
biographies or issue memoirs ; nor are their letters preserved and published for
the instruction and entertainment of posterity. Only those who, through birth
or talent or circumstance, move among the people who are "somebodies,"
and take part in social events that " count," put the story of their personal lives
into print. Apart from the oral recollections of those who lived in the latter
half of the Victorian era, the nearest one can get to a picture of social life in the
outer suburbs of the day is in such humorous, but essentially truthful, records
as *The Diary of a Nobody*.

The Nobodies of the later eighteen-hundreds gave evening parties and
impromptu suppers (at which the family had to refuse the tastiest dish for fear
there might not be enough to go round). They promenaded in the local parks
and derived amusement from the varied life of the streets, where German bands
vied in attraction with dancing bears and performing monkeys or the curious
one-man orchestra—a single performer carrying pipe, accordion, cymbals,
drum, triangle, and bells disposed about his person in such a way that, by spasmodic jerks, he contrived to play them all at once or in turn as required by the
melody of the moment. Bronzed Breton onion sellers went their rounds. The
Salvation Army girl called from house to house offering for sale calico chemises
and nightdresses made in " Army " homes of rescue. The Punch and Judy man
set up his booth on regular days of the week. Crazy evangelistic sailors out of
a berth bawled news of salvation down the middle of the road, where the milk-
man's nag trotted soberly from house to house, stopping unguided at the gate of
each customer while its master followed on foot.

The muffin man's bell rang out clear and inviting on cold winter afternoons ;
and as the shades of evening began to fall the lamplighter appeared, performing
his office swiftly, silently—a sure sign that the children's bedtime was approach-
ing. A clatter of hoofs, and the fire engine flashed by, out for a trial run. On
May Day all the nags of the neighbourhood turned out in their best and, headed
by the corporation's beautiful dray-horses, paraded the streets and gathered
in the local park where prizes were given for the best conditioned animals.

Whist drives in winter, tennis clubs in summer facilitated social intercourse
outside the home. Roller skating swept through the land in the late 'seventies,
and in the 'nineties mixed cycling clubs sprang up like mushrooms. Volun-
teering was a source of health and pleasure to many young men, headquarters
taking the place in their lives of their social superiors' clubs ; and the smart young
man—twin-soul of him who now runs madly through the land in a two-seater

motor-car—drove his pony trap at a furious pace, trying to pass everyone else on the road, to the distress of his female passengers on their precarious seats. He made great play with his whip, flourishing it from side to side, tickling up his own animal and irritating those of his fellow drivers.

Church-going and church activities—socials, amateur concerts, lectures, penny readings from Dickens and Shakespeare—were the substitute for to-day's ubiquitous music-hall performances and cinema shows. Piano- and violin-playing and songs in the drawing-room satisfied the musical needs now met by the gramophone and the wireless. Hours of work were longer, means of transport slower and fewer, leisure shorter. Many men who worked in the City walked back to their homes in Islington or Holloway, thus combining economy with exercise. On summer evenings, they spent an hour or two in their gardens, pottering about the cutting frame and tending with loving care those ordered arrangements of geraniums, fuchsias, calceolarias, and lobelia which constituted the acme of Victorian horticultural taste. On dark evenings each of them sat near the lighted lamp and read the paper aloud to his wife, who sat opposite, darning the family's old socks, knitting new ones, or doing " fancywork." The occasional country picnic or boating expedition was planned weeks in advance, and eagerly saved for and anticipated.

The Aerated Bread Company opened the first teashops in London in 1880. In the next twenty years similar catering establishments sprang up, and it became a recognised dissipation among suburban ladies to spend an afternoon looking at the big drapery shops in Oxford Street, and taking tea and cream buns at one of the new teashops. This was the average woman's first experience of restaurant life. Men took the mid-day meal in tavern or chophouse ; but women fed exclusively at home, and did all their entertaining there.

For Society, the year was divided rigidly into three sections—the London Season, the shooting season, and the hunting season. Except during April, May, June, and July, and a few weeks in late autumn, London was " empty." Blinds were drawn in the front of the house, a couple of servants acted as caretakers, and if some member of the family were compelled for any reason to be in London " out of the Season," she crept in and out of her own house as though she had no right there. The man put up at his Club.

Into the four months of the Season was crowded a round of gaiety for the " Upper Ten Thousand " such as will never be seen in London again. By the 'eighties already, agriculture had ceased to support landed proprietors ; but many of them had been wise enough to invest in industrial concerns, some had been lucky enough to discover coal or iron or both under their ancestral acres, and a few found themselves evolving into millionaires through the chance possession of land in London. American heiresses were beginning to arrive too ; and, though money without birth or breeding was insufficient as a passport to social eminence, yet the children of moneyed parents, having been through the approved mill of public school and university, were accepted, and helped to fill in the gaps left by the gradual impoverishment of the older aristocracy.

Mr. E. F. Benson's Lord Chesterford in *Dodo* is the picture of the perfect gentleman of his time : " He was very loyal, and very much devoted to what he considered his duty, which consisted in being an excellent landlord and J.P. of his county, in voting steadily for the Conservative party in the House of Lords, in giving largely and anonymously to good objects, in going to church on Sunday morning, where he sang hymns with fervour, and read lessons with respect, in managing a hunt in a liberal and satisfactory manner, and in avoiding any introspection or speculation about problems of life and being." The perfect gentleman's wife and counterpart, the perfect lady, dressed well, entertained lavishly without ostentation, was a benevolent despot to the old women of the village, and a regular attendant at church, where she withstood the rigours of the service by the aid of a vinaigrette: a necessity since tight lacing induced in every well dressed woman a tendency to faint under the stress of fatigue or emotion.

With the marriage of the Prince of Wales, Society was divided into two camps—the retired and dismal circle round the widowed Queen, and the gayer group round the Prince and his young and lovely Princess, dubbed the Marlborough House Set. The Court chronicle in the newspapers consisted of columns of such announcements as " On Wednesday the Queen, attended by the Marchioness of Ely, took a carriage drive," " H.R.H. Princess Helena went out driving attended by the Hon. Flora Macdonald." The doings of the Marlborough House Set would have made less sober reading ; and some of them were whispered rather than blazed abroad. Once, indeed, the Prince of Wales was actually summoned as a witness in a divorce case—the Mordaunt case in 1871, in which the respondent—speedily declared unfit to plead—had owned to her husband that " she had done him very wrong " with several people. The Queen was shocked and horrified. Yet, though the Prince's father had been Albert the Good, his mother was a niece of the Prince Regent.

In the early 'eighties young married women in the fashionable set were alleged to have no sense of morality. It was commonly said that women in Society were drinking to excess. Some of them had taken to cigarette smoking— a habit which, by the 'nineties, was not unusual in the privacy of the home. Make-up was discreetly advertised in ladies' papers—" Crème Admiratrice, the only preparation for restoring the clear and healthy appearance of a youthful complexion ; Veloutine powder ; eyebrow pencils ; Fard Indien in all shades for darkening and improving the eyebrows; Bâton au Raisin for the lips "—all the battery of beauty beloved of the fashionable girl in the nineteen-thirties offered to her predecessor of fifty and sixty years ago.

A group of troubled though titled ladies besought Archbishop Benson to do something to stop the moral rot which was destroying Society. The Archbishop arranged a series of devotional meetings in the chapel of Lambeth Palace which were filled to overflowing—he felt that without involving himself and the Church in the most awkward social predicament he could not do more. Even so he

VERY ROYAL ASCOT : " A brilliant sun shone on the first day at Ascot this year, and on the favourites that came home with a regularity which only book-makers found monotonous. For the first time in his career the Prince of Wales won two races in succession, which the inborn loyalty of the British subject made especially gratifying. As H.R.H.'s horses passed the Enclosure, its brilliantly coloured tenants clustered to the rails in the most charming arrangement of beauty and fashion " (1895)

earned the disfavour of the Queen, who was unable to comprehend why people of position should want to meet in public on week-days for religious exercises.

Through such cracks in the surface of Society life, it began to appear that all was not well with the social fabric, that the actual bliss of Victorian monogamic matrimony was not up to theory. All women were not by nature chaste, nor as entirely devoted to their husbands, alive or dead, as their sovereign ; all men were not monuments of noble fidelity, like the Prince Consort. The first Marriage and Divorce Act was passed in 1857 ; but women in Society rarely claimed its benefits, for to do so involved social ruin. A man known to be an unfaithful husband was, if socially eligible, received by the Queen. A woman, however innocent, was, if she had been indiscreet enough to reveal to the world the miseries of an unsatisfactory domesticity, debarred from the Royal presence, and ostracised from the social group ranged about the Queen. Not till 1887— thirty years after the passing of the Act—did Victoria, on Lord Salisbury's advice, modify her attitude towards successful women petitioners for divorce. " The fact that she has gained her suit shows that neither her husband's Counsel nor the Queen's Proctor have been able to attack it [her character]," wrote Lord Salisbury, and added, " With respect to men who have been divorced for their own adultery, Lord Salisbury would be very glad if Your Majesty should decide to give them no social recognition of any kind . . . but this would be a very considerable change."

For a number of years after the Prince Consort's death Victoria absolutely refused to hold the Drawing Rooms at which it was customary for débutantes to make their first bow to the world. After the Prince's marriage, the Princess of Wales deputised for her. But Victoria decreed that these big state gatherings should be held, not at Buckingham Palace which was renovated during the 'sixties at great expense to the public, but at St. James's Palace, as in Albert's day. It was with difficulty that the ladies in their carriages reached the entrance. It was with difficulty that they squeezed through the small rooms to the audience chamber. It was as in a nightmare that they tried to depart, for there was no system by which carriages could be timed to reach the exit at the same moment as their owners, who were waiting jammed together in a long narrow corridor with no possibility of moving forward or back faster than the mass moved. A woman might hear her carriage announced, and driven away, several times before, dishevelled and distraught, she was able to struggle to the exit ; and not so much as a cup of tea was served to the ladies to refresh them after the wearisome hours they had spent in order to pay their respects to the Queen's proxy. Even when, some years later, Victoria once more received in person, and ladies attended in more spacious Buckingham Palace to kiss Her Majesty's " small, soft, red hand," the occasions were so rare that the crowding was nearly as disagreeable. The arrangements for departure were little better—and still no refreshment was offered.

A more imaginative order ruled at Marlborough House. Not only did the Prince and his wife receive guests in the most seemly way and on all kinds of occasions, public and private, but they also accepted the hospitality of their future subjects. They attended dinners and balls in London, and paid country house visits with a freedom from etiquette and restraint which scandalised the Queen and her numerous relatives in the royal courts of Germany; but which endeared them to English people of all classes and went a long way towards removing the cloud under which royalty had fallen in popular esteem in this country through Victoria's indifference, during a quarter of a century, to the public claims of her position. With cheerful pertinacity, the Prince and Princess laid foundation stones, opened hospitals and art galleries, launched battleships, and attended charity bazaars. They were, though the Queen did not realise it, the mainstay of the social order to which she was accustomed, at a moment when republican sentiments were professed, according to some contemporary estimates, by a very vocal third of the population. People in general were weary of the drain on national resources made by the privy purse, for which there was no visible return in the form of regal pageantry. Victoria's assumption of the imperial status, so pleasing to herself, was matter of indifference to them: they wanted a Queen who would be queenly in the orthodox way.

Hyde Park in the neighbourhood of Rotten Row was the open-air centre of social life during the Season. The First Commissioner of Works in 1872 issued an order that " bath chairs and perambulators may not be brought into these walks " (the walks and avenues leading to Rotten Row) " between 11 a.m. and 2 p.m." During those hours, the fashionable quarter of the Park was reserved to Society, which came in carriages or on horseback and sat on little chairs or ambled in the Row or drove slowly up and down, smiling, bowing, chatting to friends and acquaintances. It was the time and the place for seeing and being seen.

" One ' booked ' friends for luncheon, and perhaps drove them down Piccadilly prancing on the wide sweep of pavement, glancing up at the Turf Club window as a possible place to find an extra man for a dinner party," says the Countess of Warwick, in *Life's Ebb and Flow.* " The hill down St. James's Street was a splendid show of ' spanking tits '; no interfering traffic, and only a hat-raising or bowing to friends hurrying up or down to their luncheon engagements. Late afternoon in Hyde Park meant state carriages and barouches with beautifully dressed occupants pulled up under the trees. It was not etiquette to handle the reins oneself in the afternoons, so we sat on rows of chairs chatting and behaving as if the world we knew bounded by the Smart Set was a fixed orbit, as if London—our London—was a place of select social enjoyment for the Circle, as if nothing could change in this best of delightful worlds. Then there would be a clatter of faster horses, and down this mile of drive came the well-known Royal carriage with the beautiful Alexandra, Princess of Wales, bowing right and left as only she could bow, and hats were raised and knees curtsied before seats were resumed and interrupted chatter continued."

The coming of the motor-car put an end to all that. Edward took his first motor-car drive in 1898, almost immediately after the removal of restrictions on mechanical traction on the roads, and so set the seal of social approval on the new monsters. In their heyday, horses of quality changed hands at Tattersall's for four and five hundred guineas apiece, and on the Sunday before a Monday sale a gathering assembled in the gallery at the famous horse dealer's as fashionable as an audience at the Opera.

Young men, and older ones who believed in exercise, and energetic young women rose at 8 in the morning, despite late hours the night before, and rode in the Park before breakfast. The ladies invariably rode side-saddle, in long flowing skirts and tall silk hats : the Row was sacred to men and women who were ready to dress and behave with orthodox correctitude—to whom, indeed, it would never have occurred to behave otherwise.

On Sundays, there was a regular church parade when, religious duties fulfilled by attendance at morning service, top-hatted men and women dressed in the latest modes sauntered under the trees to encourage an appetite for lunch. The week-end habit, which empties fashionable London, such as it is, on Sundays and obliterates the hard line that used to lie between living in town and living in the country has killed this weekly spectacle, as well as the drives by coach to Hurlingham and the water parties at Richmond which were Society's only recognition of country delights at the sweetest time of the year.

Throughout the period, there was Art, represented principally by the Royal Academy, where All That Was Best in the pictures of the day was infallibly garnered (and found a ready sale) year by year. Gigantic " masterpieces " by Alma Tadema, Landseer, and Leighton, which now, when put up to auction, fetch scarcely the value of their canvas, paint, and frames, were bought by their makers' delighted contemporaries for hundreds and sometimes thousands of pounds. It was, after all, the period in which the *Daily Telegraph* described the Albert Memorial as " assuredly the most consummate and elegant piece of elegiac art which modern genius has produced . . . indeed a possession which ennobles the capital." The age was opulent, and so were its famous artists, in their lives and in their works.

The Grosvenor Gallery, where Rossetti and his fellow pre-Raphaelites exhibited, and later the New Gallery, to which they moved after the Grosvenor closed in 1888, were centres of a more advanced taste where the opening day of a new exhibition was a social event. Another haunt of artistic London was the Doré Gallery in Bond Street where Monsieur Gustave Doré, whose bent was the production of religious problem pictures that exactly suited the current taste, had a permanent exhibition of his works. This amazing establishment was open all the year round, and was eagerly patronised at a shilling a head.

If money were the only criterion, Doré was one of the greatest artists the world has ever seen, for the fortune he made surpassed those amassed by his most successful contemporaries.

Entertaining, which till the very end of the century took place exclusively in the home, began at breakfast time and went on to the small hours of the following morning. Breakfast invitations were especially popular among people who leavened their social activities by the exercise of a profession or by assiduous attendance at public or charitable committees. The hour appointed varied between 8.30 and 10, and the function did not last long. Guests left promptly after the meal—a custom which alone made it possible to give breakfasts and lunches without too great inroads on the day's other activities. Invitation lunches were longer and more formal than to-day's dinners. They ran into several courses, with wines to match. Five o'clock tea was the moment of informal calls, with impromptu music and a probable exhibition of the " womanly virtue of piano playing."

Dinner was the vital moment in the day—no casual telephoned invitation affair, but a carefully thought out selection of guests, food, and wine. It was by the success of her dinners that the great hostess was recognised. Invitations were for 8 or 8.30, and it was an understood convention that one arrived exactly fifteen minutes later than the time specified. The meal served was long and lavish. Diners were offered a choice of two soups, one thick, one clear—the latter well fortified with sherry. Then came fish, and perhaps a second fish, entrées—a choice of four, two brown and two white ; a joint, then poultry or game, and perhaps both ; a choice of several substantial puddings and fancy sweets, followed by cheese and finally dessert. Until the 'eighties, claret was the favoured wine. But towards the end of the century, under the guidance of the Prince of Wales's taste, champagne came to be regarded as the only possible drink at evening functions—so much so that the single word " wine " was generally understood to mean champagne in later Victorian days. There was a noticeable rise in the consumption of port during the 'nineties— over a third more was imported in 1898 than in 1884.

Dessert over, the hostess caught the eyes of the ladies. They rose as one body, made their way to the drawing-room, and there gossiped in a desultory way until joined by the men, who had been left to partake of their port or claret and indulge in masculine subjects of conversation unhindered by the presence of the ladies. It has been said that such jokes as were exchanged were of a mildness that would bring a blush of disappointed surprise to the cheek of a maiden of the nineteen-thirties. But no man has put them on record, and no woman ever heard them.

Smoking was no new vice in the 'sixties ; but until the Prince of Wales introduced the habit of cigarette smoking immediately after dinner, nicotine was not imbibed with the port. No gentleman would have thought of smoking

TEA WITH THE VOLUNTEERS: "Again we find ourselves at Wimbledon camp. We were engaged to dine with the London Scottish, but had undertaken an afternoon visit to a friend's tent; so thither we went, and found his sister and cousin brewing his camp-fire tea" (1870)

"CAMBRIDGE WINS: English women of all orders are enthusiastic admirers of pluck, and it is the spectacle of muscular courage which attracts thousands of ladies to the Boat Race. Many a respectable matron gives herself up to mad applause and wild fervour" (1870)

"DARWINIAN THEORY : A cage of monkeys has intense interest. We can see ourselves, bereft of speech and furnished with tails, but otherwise remarkably human. But do the Zoological Garden monkeys consider our modern, civilised selves to be at all simian ? " (1871)

in garments in which he would subsequently join the ladies—in those days prone to faint at the slightest whiff of the noxious weed. Until after the marriage of her youngest daughter Beatrice, the " Perpetual Princess," to Prince Henry of Battenberg, Queen Victoria allowed no smoking in any of the royal residences. The Prince of Wales was once confined to his room for a month for transgressing this rule. Until the introduction of the cigarette, most ladies followed the Queen's example, and the gentlemen, if they wished to smoke, had to don their frogged smoking jackets and embroidered smoking caps and retire to the garden or to the gun-room or some other remote corner of the house where females never penetrated. It was the cigarette which overcame feminine resistance to such good (or bad) purpose that the ladies themselves, before the century was out, fell victims to the habit.

After dinner, more guests arrived at ten for an informal evening gathering— delightfully christened by Mary Gladstone a " tail "—at which, while some discussed the most recent frontier war or the latest scandal, others played whist. In the drawing-room there was music—Albani or some other singer from the opera, or Mr. George Santley, who sang so finely in oratorio ; or there might be an entertainer of the calibre of Albert Chevalier with his Cockney songs.

Sometimes the dinner party migrated to a ball or a less formal dance, where the waltz, danced very fast and without reversing, went on till four o'clock in the morning, varied now and again by a polka, and an occasional set dance— the Lancers or a Cotillion, to which new figures were continually being added. It was not the exclusive prerogative of hostesses to give balls. Men gave them too. There was a Bachelors' Ball during the Season, and the balls given by the Blues and the Life Guards were famous for the fine dancing to be seen there. Sometimes the cry was raised that balls were going out of fashion, that young people preferred drinking tea at a kettledrum or sitting through a penny reading ; but the prophets of gloom were never justified ; and the young continued to whirl away the hours in the waltz.

Every night of the Season the Opera at Covent Garden was crowded with bejewelled and fashionable beauty. The ballets at the old Empire and at the Alhambra ran their course through the seasons. Henry Irving and Ellen Terry filled the Lyceum. Mrs. Langtry, dressed in the height of fashion, roused excited admiration of her loveliness in plays by Pinero, Oscar Wilde, and less distinguished authors. Yvette Guilbert and Sarah Bernhardt enlivened the native theatre by occasional brief visits. The Albert Hall was crammed to capacity for performances of Haydn's *Creation* or Handel's *Messiah*. Mme. Tussaud's Waxworks was a universally popular show. The Shah of Persia was taken there by underground in 1873. He was also taken to the Crystal Palace, of which building, and the entertainments it housed, the Victorian public was prouder than of any other monument of the age. He exclaimed after his visit, " C'était la plus heureuse soirée que j'ai gouté en Europe," so perhaps the public was justified in its view.

A FAMILY PARTY FOR DRURY LANE PANTOMIME (1870)

MADEMOISELLE NILSSON'S FAREWELL : " In spite of unkind critics and hints about a weakened voice, Mademoiselle Nilsson has been a great favourite this year. For her last unmarried appearance the choice was Gounod's Faust, in which the statuesque Swede is superb " (1872)

" AT THE OPERA: We cannot help expressing dissatisfaction with the length of the skirts trailing on the steps of the Opera staircase. Either you must remove them as delicately as may be with your foot, or else you must tread on them. In fact, to persons who go to the Opera for the music, the horrid trouble of getting away interferes with the evening's pleasure " (1870)

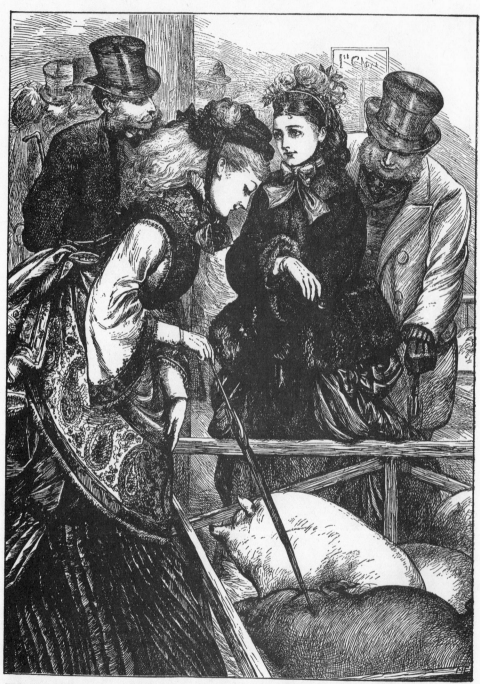

PIG-PRODDING : " The Agricultural Hall is always thronged for the annual Cattle Show. The judges begin their work of inspection at nine o'clock, but it was at a later hour that the fair visitor of our sketch made her parasol-inspection of the pigs, which this year fall below the average " (1871)

" THE METROPOLITAN HORSE SHOW : Country folk in the Agricultural Hall hang round some well-known hunter, but London visitors prefer a pet pony or high-stepping hack " (1870)

" THE HORTICULTURAL GARDENS : The Great Rose Show of the South Kensington season was a success, the company, including splendidly dressed Asiatics, vying with the flowers " (1872)

"RINKOMANIA: The Princes Cricket and Skating Club consists of ladies and gentlemen of rank and position, and is very exclusive. Some men have attained great proficiency with wheeled skates, but the ladies go in for gentle exercise. There is a slight loss of ladylike complacency among female beginners, but none are so ill-bred as to remark their tumbles" (1875)

ROTTEN ROW : " The greater part of the crowd in mid-season consists of that fashionable world which is known to the public only in the aggregate ; a stream of gentlemen who all look gallant, thanks very often to their tailors' skill, and of ladies who all look beautiful, in spite of the prevailing Mode's extravagances " (1871)

THE DUCHESS'S BALL : " The utmost hilarity and vivacity prevailed at the Duchess of Argyll's Grand Ball. The Princess Louise (Marchioness of Lorne) took her share with the best imaginable good humour, and stayed into the small hours " (1871)

A MASONIC BALL.: "This ball was given by the Isaac Newton University Lodge of Freemasons in Cambridge. The first quadrille was danced by all the brethren in craft aprons. The members of the higher degrees afterwards assumed their respective dresses, separate sets of Lancers being alloted to the Mark Masters and Royal Ark Mariners, the Royal Arch, the Rose Croix, the Knights Templar, and the Knights of Malta. The engraving represents the third figure of the Knights Templar's Lancers" (1876)

CRYSTAL PALACE LORE: " You may enjoy an unrivalled prospect from the Grand Saloon Dining Room in the Crystal Palace. Fountains spout silvery streams, and indigo tints from summer night are lit up by the firework festival's glories. The price of dinner is from five shillings to four guineas. A second-class dinner for humbler customers is twenty pence, a third-class one, beer included, being half that amount " (1870)

GLADSTONES AT HOME: " Everyone enjoyed the mixed reading from Shakespeare and Macaulay given recently by Mr. Pennington, the Shakespearean actor, at Mr. W. E. Gladstone's house in Carlton House Terrace. Mrs. and the Misses Gladstone received the guests, but Mr. Gladstone stood the whole time in the doorway with arms folded " (1872)

"THE GROSVENOR GALLERY: The object of Sir Coutts Lindsay in erecting this building was to afford to pictures and sculptures the advantages they receive in private houses from a background of harmoniously patterned walls and appropriate furniture. The entrance in New Bond Street is by an imposing façade of stone in Renaissance style, with a fine doorway formerly belonging to the Church of Santa Lucia at Venice " (1877)

"A ROYAL BRIDE'S ROSES : The Duke of Connaught and Princess Louise Margaret, with her father, Prince Frederick Charles, arrived at Dover from Ostend by special steamer. The Royal party lunched at the Lord Warden Hotel, and the Princess, who wore a hat and jacket of black silk and a grey costume, was presented by Miss Swainson, daughter of the proprietor, with a magnificent bouquet of roses " (1878)

MADAME ALBANI SINGING "THE LAST ROSE OF SUMMER" BEFORE MEMBERS
AND CHORISTERS OF THE IMPERIAL RUSSIAN COURT (1874)

" THE PRINCESS'S OWN : The Princess of Wales made a neat little speech to officers and men of the 19th Regiment (1st York North Riding) when presenting their new colours to kneeling officers in Sheffield. Before their Royal Highnesses left, the Princess expressed a wish that the Regiment should be known in future as the Princess of Wales's own ". (1875)

THE PRINCE AND PRINCESS OF WALES RECEIVING GUESTS AT A GARDEN PARTY AT MARLBOROUGH HOUSE (1878)

MRS. LANGTRY'S DRESSES: "From an early point in *The Fringe of Society* at the Criterion, it was evident that the audience felt no deep interest in the various personages. Mrs. Langtry, attired in a succession of gowns which excited the admiration of the ladies in the stalls, played the part of the temptress with success" (1892)

"THE WANING HONEYMOON: Those persons who have experienced a *lune de miel* know that there is a risk in suddenly placing two people in constant, isolated companionship for thirty days. Rapid travelling produces fatigue, and the couple who exchanged vows of everlasting love may be just a *leetle* bit weary of each other" (1883)

" AFTER THE PLAY : One always feels disillusioned on leaving the theatre. In our picture the weather is fine, but when it is not, those going by cab or private carriage feel the benefit of the ample portico at the Lyceum " (1881)

A FUTURE QUEEN OF SPAIN: "The Infant Princess of Battenberg was christened in the Drawing-Room at Balmoral Castle. Queen Victoria entered with the Prince and Princess Henry of Battenberg, and the service commenced with a choral composed by the Prince Consort. The infant, who received the names of Victoria Eugénie Julia Ena, was handed to the Queen, who at once transferred it to the officiating minister. The water used for the Baptism came specially from the River Jordan" (1887)

PRINCESS AND SHAH: " The comparatively small gardens of the Prince of Wales's town house looked their best for the garden-party given for the Shah of Persia. The Queen received His Serene Majesty, who beckoned the Princess of Wales, who clearly pleases him, to sit by his side, and attempted to express his thoughts by means of those curious pantomimic actions which of late have so often been seen to cause an almost embarrassing amusement to Her Royal Highness " (1889)

AT BURLINGTON HOUSE : " The Royal Academy Exhibition has become a favourite resort of both the fashionable and the unfashionable worlds. Now that the means of locomotion have so largely increased, country cousins make a point of running up to town to ' see the Academy,' and the merits or demerits of the various ' Millais ' or ' Leightons ' furnish food for their local discussion during months afterwards. Although the Exhibition has been moved from the cramped quarters of a wing of the National Gallery to the spacious rooms in Burlington House, it is always crowded to excess with a motley throng ". (1880)

"CHURCH PARADE: There is no better opportunity of studying *le dernier cri* than that which the Park affords, between half-past twelve and two o'clock on any fine Sunday in July. Women may have Ascot or Goodwood in mind when they order some particularly striking toilette, but they will wear it all the same in the Park; while those who have been bidden to wedding receptions and at homes, to concerts and fêtes, will also don their dressmakers' triumphs for Church Parade" (1892)

" THE VICEROY'S SALUTE: Lord and Lady Zetland held their first Levée and Drawing Room in Dublin Castle last week, which were very brilliant affairs. These differ from the similar ceremonies in England in the manner of greeting the debutantes. It is not the least pleasant of the Viceroy's duties to kiss each blushing beauty on the cheek as she is presented " (1891)

A SOULFUL EVENT : " To the girl who kisses the Queen's hand, and by so doing marks her entry into the great world, the day is only second in importance to that of her marriage. All her soul is centred on her curtsey, on kissing Her Majesty's hand, and on backing gracefully out of the presence without forgetting any of the Royalties present, and without looking awkward " (1893)

FÊTE CHAMPÊTRE : " More than 20,000 of Clarke's Fairy lamps were picturesquely used in decorating the gardens of the Royal Botanic Society in the Regent's Park for the annual evening fête. Long avenues were lighted by festoons of gas jets enclosed in opalescent globes ; while at intervals coloured fires blazed forth. A thousand Fairy lamps were also used in the Conservatory. Three bands performed, the Royal Hand-Bell Ringers also attended, and the London Male Voice Club was heard on the lake " (1887)

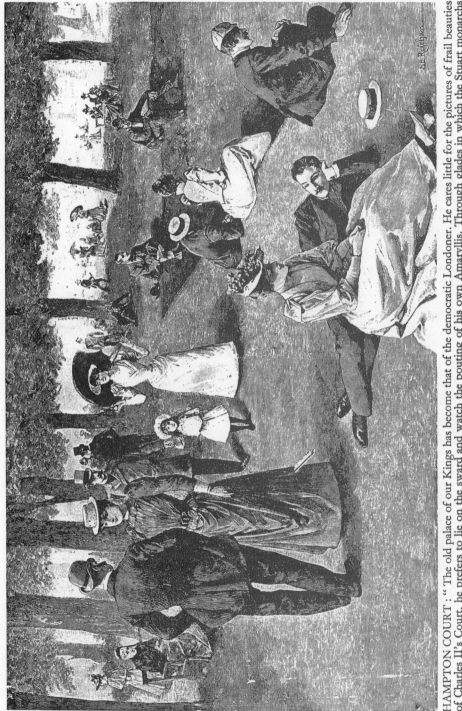

HAMPTON COURT: " The old palace of our Kings has become that of the democratic Londoner. He cares little for the pictures of frail beauties of Charles II's Court, he prefers to lie on the sward and watch the pouting of his own Amaryllis. Through glades in which the Stuart monarchs took delight 'Arry and 'Arriet wander unconcernedly " (1891)

MUSIC HATH SOUNDS : " No step taken within recent years to brighten London has been more widely appreciated than the introduction of bands into public parks. It is only necessary to see the faces of the crowd round the band stand in Hyde Park to know how the boon is valued " (1895)

" PONY RACING FOR LADIES : For some at Hurlingham there is pigeon shooting, for
others polo, and then there is pony racing, which the ladies love best—the ponies are small
and therefore appeal to the feminine heart " (1890)

" A PARADE OF AUTO-MOTOR CARS : The exhibition of horseless carriages at the Imperial Institute shows the leading makes at work. Among them are the much-vaunted Kane-Pennington motor-carriage from America, a couple of Daimler motor-cars, the Lutzmann carriage, the Dion-Bouton and the Bollée, the latter a tandem, which ran with ease and speed " (1896)

FLUNKEYS AT TEATIME: " At the doors of the confectioners' shops in Regent Street may be seen little knots of footmen and pages waiting while mistresses enjoy their tea inside. The young lads, fresh from the country, gaze with wonder and delight at the pastrycook's art in the windows, and form a contrast to the older servants, whose air is one of boredom" (1898)

THE PRINCE THANKS MR. TATE.: "The opening ceremony of the extension of the National Gallery, made possible by Mr. Tate's generosity, took place in the room where hang the sixty-five pictures given by Mr. Tate. In the group which ranged themselves on a little platform placed immediately beneath Lord Leighton's picture, 'The Sea shall give up its Dead,' were the Prince and Princess of Wales, the Duke and Duchess of York, the Duke and Duchess of Fife, the trustees (Lord Lansdowne, the Earl of Carlisle, Lord Brownlow, Mr. Alfred Rothschild, Sir Charles Tenant, Mr. J. P. Heseltine, and Mr. Murray Scott), and Mr. and Mrs. Tate." (1897)

II

"THE ENGLISH LIVE AT HOME"

In no age, in no country has the home meant as much as it did to the Victorians. "Woman's place is the home" had been a sentiment common hitherto to every age; but during the Victorian era man's place was the home too. Inside the home man was expected to find his relaxation and pleasure. Clubs were for those of social pretensions only, Sunday golf was not yet, and the average middle class man spent his life oscillating between his home and his office or factory with the regularity of the pendulum in his own well-timed grandfather clock.

This worship of the home, rooted in the reaction that naturally followed the drunken libertinism of the Regency and George IV's reign, had begun to spring up under William IV and his homely Queen Adelaide. It received a great impetus from the wholesome home life of Victoria and her Consort: a manifestation of virtue in high circles due no doubt in large measure to Albert's placid temperament where the female sex was concerned. But in 1870, Albert had been dead nine years, the Queen was still resolute in her refusal to please the public with her presence, and the freer life of Marlborough House set the tone in fashionable Society: another reaction was in process of birth.

Not that the change was noticeable in any but a certain limited group. The whole of the middle class, from the lower ranks of the aristocracy to the poorest suburban clerk, was still steeped in the Victorian mood.

The Victorian home owed its equilibrium to two things: an implicit faith in the indissolubility of marriage, and an unshakable belief in the Pauline doctrine of woman's inferiority: a belief by no means peculiar to men—women held it with equal tenacity. On those who were well mated, these faiths sat lightly. It was the ill mated—and the unmated—who were finally to upset the balance of Victorian values.

The outstanding feature of the later Victorian home was the size of the families—birth control even by self control had not so much as crossed the thoughts of the hardest pressed father: would it not have meant a gross interference with his legitimate pleasures in the married state? And if his wife died in the weariness of childbed, as the great popularity of "orphan" songs in the drawing-room emphasises was the case, she could easily be replaced, since marriage was the only career, at once remunerative and respectable, open to the middle-class woman. And when the family ceased to live under one roof— as even in Victorian days they inevitably did (unless the family consisted of a long row of unhandsome and undowried daughters)—their effigies adorned the walls, the piano top, and the mantelpiece, and lay piled up in albums upon the drawing-room table. For photography came pat upon its time to put on record the features of their innumerable progeny for the solace of bleeding hearts perforce parted from their young.

OUR MOTHERS

Round the solid mahogany breakfast table sat the Victorian father and mother with their graduated family—one, two, three, four—each year a new face added to the board. Industry was booming, trade was soaring, the markets of the world seemed insatiable. Even where there was racking anxiety and an endless strain to keep up those appearances so essential to genteel life and happiness, success and sufficiency were only just round the corner, and one would certainly not offend the Lord and renounce all hope of His ultimate bounty by questioning His wisdom in sending still another small mouth to feed, another small body to be clothed and shod, with a mind somehow to be educated. It is true that what the Lord gave He frequently took away—a gossip writer of 1871, referring to the recovery of the Prince of Wales from a serious illness, remarks in the most matter-of-fact way, " We need not here dwell on the fact of the happy marriage of the Prince and Princess, except to observe that hitherto all their children have been spared to them except the infant, John Alexander, to whom a monument is erected in Sandringham churchyard." One small corpse among five living children was so moderate a proportion that the parents should consider themselves fortunate. Official figures show that sixty infants in every thousand under five were carried off annually (the corresponding rate in 1930 was 18.3). But, again, who dare question the Lord's inscrutable wisdom ? Woman was made to be man's comfort and to bear his children, and bear them she should and did.

Those who survived the perils of babyhood—in the late 'seventies no English perambulator was made in which the infant could lie down—had reason to thank the fate which had put them into big families. The average child of the Victorian age had little prospect of sympathy and understanding if these did not come from its contemporaries in the nursery. The adult attitude to the child is typified by this chance remark in an article on children's books : " One great fault of children's books as a class is that they are about children who are made to appear martyrs, geniuses, *personages*. Little boys and girls ought not to regard themselves, as these stories teach them to do, as possible personages. . . . They should be left to the happy humility of unspoiled children who do not discover that they are worth thinking about."

The natural result of such an attitude was that, wherever house accommodation was ample and service plentiful, the children were left much to one another and to the haphazard care and affection of that other despised caste, the servants. Among these dwellers in attic and basement, they felt happy. Such conditions ruled in a far larger proportion of middle class families then than they do to-day. Service was cheap, and rents were low—one-tenth was, in general, the maximum proportion of the income allotted to rent. Mr. E. F. Benson relates of his father that as a young student he was given by his mother a big empty room in her house : she was able to spare him this space despite the fact that she was a widow with seven children to bring up whose unworldly husband had died at forty-two leaving her " an inconveniently small income."

When children made their brief emergences into the parental life—at

" THE NEW CURATE : Eager curiosity over the new curate is inevitable among the softer sex. Possibly he may become somebody's life-partner, and certainly he will be their associate, if at all an eligible gentleman, in charitable organisations, as well as in croquet or lawn-tennis. This curate is an excellent specimen of the fresh-coloured youth who feels shy under keen female eyes " (1876)

" A MUSICAL REHEARSAL : Mothers who teach the pianoforte have a hard battle. During months of drudgery the keys are rendered sticky by childish tears. But a rich reward follows the repulsive scale period. The boy may not turn out a Paganini, but he is sure to be in request in musical drawing-rooms " (1872)

" MAMMA'S BIRTHDAY : This engraving represents a domestic scene enacted in every family.
Breakfast is over, Mamma is sitting unoccupied. Now is the time for the children's deeply matured
scheme. Nelly, the youngest girl, presents a bouquet and reads a birthday poem, while Mary
anxiously watches the effect in Mamma's face and Harry represses his excitement in the background.
Meanwhile Papa smiles benignly over his newspaper " (1872)

breakfast, at the mid-day meal, and for a short while before their bedtime—they lived under a sense of strain. Their elders were creatures of unaccountable moods. A burst of laughter, a tear, an irrepressible attack of animal high spirits which might at one time be indulgently received would at another bring instant banishment to the nursery, and the forfeiture of one's pudding. It was the child's duty to be seen occasionally and heard rarely. It is not to be wondered at that children returned to the freedom of contacts among the maidservants with a feeling of glad relief; and that, when they were fortunate enough to have a devoted nurse such as is idealised in more than one book of memoirs of the period, they adored her. These marvellously unselfish beings stayed with a family from generation to generation, having no ties or desires of their own. Devoted absolutely to their young charges, and to their children in turn, at last, worn out in faithful service, they sometimes (but not always) received their earthly reward in a tiny pension, and perhaps a room and attendance in the house they had made home for its youthful inmates.

From the nursery, children passed to the schoolroom, where an untrained governess, whose wages were probably less than those of the cook, tried to teach them subjects she had never been properly taught herself—reading, writing, and a smattering of arithmetic and French, and, for the girls, sewing, music, and watercolour drawing. There were good governesses, just as there were enlightened and understanding parents who really enjoyed the society of their children : but a majority of governesses were inefficient because their employers were unable to offer a sufficient wage to make efficiency a profitable acquisition. Some girls reached boarding school. If they were lucky, they found themselves at Cheltenham or some other of the new schools for girls run on public school lines. The boys migrated, as a matter of course, to preparatory and public schools, for they had careers to make ; whereas the girls had merely to wait at home for the husband who would turn up providentially at the right moment.

Moral persuasion was of little account in the nursery or schoolroom. There were certain dogmas of conduct, certain musts and must-nots which it was demanded that the child should respect and obey. Canings and slappings were the recognised mode of correcting failure to comply with the canons of behaviour laid down. Queen Victoria was a firm believer in this form of discipline, which she is said to have used once on her grandson, the ex-Kaiser, in his childhood when he was staying with her and refused to do as he was bid.

Sundays were days of torment for the young. Dressed in their best clothes, they were forbidden to play, with toys or without them—though in some families Noah's Ark was allowed, in deference to its Bible associations. Story books, although the large majority aimed at instilling moral precepts or religious dogmas, were laid aside. Instead into the children's innocent hands was put a book on the Collects, *The Pilgrim's Progress*, or even the Holy Bible. Attendance at church and Sunday-school was rigorously enforced. There was an unwonted show of willingness for bed at the close of this dreariest of days.

Children made their own entertainment. They had so many cousins, with whom they exchanged visits, that contacts with children outside the family were rare and not much sought. Once a year small town-dwellers were taken to the pantomime, where their unsophisticated minds found material for weeks of day-dreaming in transformation scenes and Harlequinades which would reduce many a child of the nineteen-thirties to tearful boredom.

The children of the poorer middle class lacked the great boon of isolation from unsympathetic elders enjoyed by those better off. Once their nursery days were over (a mother who did not keep at least a nurse-maid for her babies was scarcely middle class) and they began to go to day schools, they spent their evenings herded together in one room with their parents. A writer in 1884 laments the injury done to young people's health by the worry and dissatisfaction entailed in having to prepare lessons in the common sitting-room, where their elders engaged in reading, conversation, sewing, fretwork, and other hobbies, and their juniors in pre-bedtime games. " Want of quietude compels them to pore over their books till long after they ought to be in bed." But the child who tried to escape to solitude was regarded as peculiar, if not vicious, and was promptly pursued and brought back to the family circle.

The hearty breakfast over, papa disappeared, either into his study or to his office ; the children went off to the nursery or the schoolroom ; mamma consulted with the cook as to the unexciting meals of the day, superintended other household matters, and wrote letters ; while the domestics scattered to their appointed tasks. The mid-day meal, which was lunch for the grown-ups and dinner for the children, was served at two, at which hour papa, if he was in the City, consumed his chop or steak and porter at his favourite chophouse. If there were guests, or the income were large, the customary meat with potatoes, followed by a sweet, was expanded into a three, four, or five course meal. An American who visited England in 1875–6 commented with surprise on the absence of napkins at lunch, though they were customary at dinner. At five o'clock mamma took afternoon tea, consisting of tea, very thin bread-and-butter, and light cakes. There might be callers ; when, if the family boasted adolescent or adult daughters, there was a little music, including a song or two, as entertainment. At six came the nursery high-tea-supper ; and at eight or half past, to suit papa's convenience, dinner was served, in a style in keeping with the pretensions of the family. In many households, a light supper was served at about ten.

The adults of the family retired to rest at eleven in bedrooms where the windows had been closed, the shutters fastened, and the curtains drawn hours before. Many housewives never read, and therefore never acted upon, the following advice on fresh air published anonymously in 1868. After dilating on the dangers of inhaling carbonic acid gas and decomposing animal exhalations from the skin and lungs, and the consequent necessity for a change of air, the writer concludes : " The immediate object of this article is to impress on all

" THE CHRISTMAS POSTMAN : Here is the rural postman, and here is a young lady of tender years, begging, like a four-footed creature, for a letter. As for her elders, they are equally expectant, though less demonstrative " (1872)

THE PRINCE AND PRINCESS OF WALES AND THEIR CHILDREN: George Frederick Ernest Albert [King George V], Victoria Alexandra Olga Mary, Maud Charlotte Mary Victoria [Queen of Norway], Albert Victor Christian Edward [died 1892], Louise Victoria Alexandra Dagmar [Princess Royal and Duchess of Fife, died 1930] (1871)

persons the extreme desirability "—no, not of opening the windows, but—"of leaving the fireplace open in all sleeping rooms. Many persons forget the necessity for fresh air, and close the fireplaces with a chimney board immediately on the advent of cold weather."

From a night spent in this close confinement, the family rose again ; and before the first too, too solid meal of the day, family and domestics filed into the dining-room, and family prayers were said—all too often long, dreary petitions by an uninspired predicant to a dreary deity whose main preoccupation appeared to be to prevent people, and especially women and children, from enjoying under any pretext the most innocent pleasures of idleness. It was the only moment during the long day when domestics were recognised by their employers as beings capable of salvation.

Domestics, in the plural, there commonly were, for to keep but one was the last stigma of genteel poverty—even the widowed mamma of the famous little Lord Fauntleroy, typical of her day, kept a maid and a nurse, though left in the direst straits. And, indeed, it cost but little to maintain a couple of maids in the 'seventies when £15–£20 a year was a good wage, and when, according to a household authority writing in 1871, in a " family where economy, with due regard to health, is the first object " the cost of each person for food and washing " must not exceed 10s. a week." The best parts of beef and mutton cost 9½d. a pound, the cheapest 3½d. Australian preserved meat was beginning to find its way into English homes where, though it was not so well liked as fresh meat, it was found palatable enough when cold. An actual budget of the day[1] for master, mistress, two daughters, and two servants in a family where " every economy is practised and few visitors are entertained " (oh, happy phrase !) gives the following figures for food and washing in two consecutive weeks : washing, 7s. 6d. ; vegetables, 3s. 6d. ; butcher, 19s. ; grocer, 9s. 6d. ; baker, 6s. 5d. ; milk, 4s. 4d. ; butterman, 5s. ; total £2 15s. Second week : washing, 7s. 1d. ; vegetables, 2s. 10d. ; butcher, 18s. 8d. ; grocer, 9s. ; baker, 6s. 2d. ; milk, 4s. 8d. ; butterman, 11s. 10d. : total, £3 0s. 3d. The expenditure on meat, in view of its low price, seems startlingly high, particularly in comparison with that on vegetables, and gives one an immediate insight into the type of diet provided—meat or bacon three times a day, and little or no fresh fruit. Butter was 1s. 3d. a pound, milk 4d. a quart, and bread 7d. a quartern.

Many women made their own and their children's clothes, despite the fantastic complexity of their styles. It was not unknown, indeed, for a girl of the 'nineties to " run up " a dress in a day. Not one of the simple frocks of yesteryear (which were little more than elaborated sacks), but a dress with leg-o'-mutton sleeves, boned and lined fitting bodice, and four-yard-round gored

[1] From the *Queen*, Feb. 18th, 1871.

skirt braided at the bottom. They made their husbands' shirts, too—at least some of them, and they used the daintiest hand stitchery in perfecting these precious garments. Long years passed before that American invention, the sewing-machine, found favour with the English housewife. " Ladies generally decide that ' they don't like sewing-machine work,' and it is said that in America, where its use is general, the only result has been that ladies put forty or fifty tucks where two or three large ones were put before," wrote Mary Taylor about 1870.

Having ordered her household and clothed herself and her family, the house-wife could still not consider her leisure well earned, and enjoy it. Serious read-ing was almost unknown among women, though Mr. Mudie's beneficent circulating libraries enabled good wives and mothers and their daughters to read, at a minimum of expense, the latest three volume romance by Rhoda Broughton or Miss Braddon, depicting the trials and tribulations and ultimate rewards of ladylike heroines. But reading was an indulgence to be used spar-ingly. A woman's hands, not her head, should be occupied ; and occupied they were, with interminable lengths of crochet and tatting, and masses of em-broidery and woolwork of stereotyped design and crushing uselessness. A woman writing in the late 'sixties put the position tersely : " With everlastingly something in their hand, no one profits by their labour, and they are reduced to look for their sole reward in civil speech made for useless gifts, or insincere praise of household ornaments that are in everybody's way." But alas these wise words went unheeded, and many weary years were to roll by before the virtuous female could abandon fancy work for healthy occupation and healthy recreation. Dr. Wingfield Stratford suggests in *The Victorian Tragedy* that the making of endless cross-stitch by the women of last century was no less pro-ductive an occupation than the cutting of divots by the woman of to-day. The trouble about it was that it was so extremely productive. The divots are re-placed and all is as though the player had never passed ; whereas the cross-stitch left behind traces that were only too visible.

The Victorian home, like the Victorian female body, was well covered, and like the Victorian female mind it was filled to overflowing with small super-fluities. Sweeping window curtains, three deep, heavy portières, long lace cur-tains to adorn the folding doors, or the space where they ought to have been, between the parlour and the drawing-room ; elaborate fringed draperies over the mantelpiece to match the heavily fringed tablecloth of sombre hue, draperies behind the piano, over the screen—wherever a drapery could be draped, there it hung. Muslins fluttered round mirrors, round the head of the matrimonial bed, round the dressing table. There must have been something hypnotic in those immense rolls of machine-made cloth, so cheap and still so new, which com-pelled women to buy yards and yards and yards of it.

Dark, dull, and expensive papers covered the walls downstairs, fidgety

" IN THE SCULLERY : Students at the new National Training School for Cookery are taught how to lay and light a fire, scour a frying pan, burnish copper saucepans and many other humble parts of kitchen education. After they have thoroughly passed through this stage, they are relegated to the hand of professed cooks " (1874)

" PRACTICAL COOKERY : Every young woman who enters the National Training School for Cookery pays two guineas, which is supposed to cover the expense of the materials she uses in learning to cook. She is taught to make soups, entrées, jellies, omelettes and everything else essential to the tables of the well-bred " (1874)

"FLIRTATION *v.* DANCING : There comes a period when the dancing grows languid and side-couples for quadrilles are in urgent request. Observing that, in spite of the powerful fingers of her professional pianist, the room is comparatively deserted, the hostess discovers a colonisation of the staircase, where couples are roosting, if we may venture on the expression, almost up to the nursery door, and where, to the accompaniment of ices and suchlike condiments, delightful confidences are exchanged " (1876)

flower patterns in cheap, quickly fading colours brightened the bedrooms. The paint was generally a uniform dull brown, grained with much skill and dexterity by a workman wielding a " comb."

The furniture, when it was not heavy, was a mass of extraneous detail. In the dining-room a large mirrored overmantel, or " chimney glass," framed in massive mahogany reflected the solid mahogany table, sideboards, and chairs. In the drawing-room, fancy ran riot. The smaller chimney glass was set in a framework of little shelves for knick-knacks. An enormous clock in white marble, flanked by pairs of massive vases, bronze figures in armour, and tall ornaments of crystal drops that matched the spreading chandelier adorned the mantelpiece. Stuffed birds, wax flowers under glass domes, occasional tables loaded with albums containing family photographs, chairs of every size (but doubtful ease) ; a horsehair sofa of repellent aspect and unmitigated discomfort ; stools and firescreens painstakingly worked in petit point or embroidered patchwork ; cabinets, what-nots, fancy shelves supported by fancy brackets all loaded with china vases and mementoes ; a grand piano in walnut, or a " cottage " in rosewood with openwork front picked out in bright pink silk ; walls covered with willow patterned plates and dishes, reproductions of Sir Edwin Landseer's stags or Sir Frederick Leighton's Greek beauties, chromolithographs of the Alps, and such family photographs as had not already found a place on piano or mantelpiece, or in an album : such was the contents of an average Victorian drawing-room of the 'seventies and 'eighties.

The bedroom was equally over-furnished—a typical suite of the period is reproduced on page 72. In 1886 a leading London firm advertised a " White Bedroom Suite, tastefully decorated with Blue or Pink, and comprising Wardrobe with Plate Glass Door, Washstand with Marble Top, Toilet Table, Large Chest of Drawers, Toilet Glass, Three Chairs, Pedestal Cupboard and Toilet Airer " for £8 15s. It will be observed that the most important item in the bedroom outfit—the ubiquitous double bed—is not included in the suite. Nor is it, from reasons of natural delicacy, reproduced in the illustrations of bedrooms of the period.

By the 'nineties things were changing. Young brides insisted on fumed oak instead of mahogany ; families were beginning to shrink and the dining table rarely needed more than one " leaf," except to accommodate company. Wallpapers were brighter, draperies less in evidence, knick-knacks less abundant, the whole aspect of the home soberer and simpler, though without distinction. William Morris had not preached his gospel of beauty in common things altogether in vain.

The home of the 'seventies and 'eighties, filled with an ever increasing family and a multiplicity of needless, and needlessly fussy, furniture and ornaments, was constructed on the basis of a tacit assumption that society was stable. It might progress—" it is a time of rapid progress," said Gladstone in 1879, " and rapid progress in itself is a good." But progress was one thing, change quite another, and unthinkable. One of the essential facts of this stable society was the constant supply of cheap and willing domestic labour. Without that, the Victorian home could not continue. And already in the 'seventies this keystone of the edifice was slipping out of place. Mrs. Augusta Webster, an ardent advocate of woman's suffrage, remarks severely that " in 1878 the servants like a long night's rest, and they like it to begin late."

That servants were beginning to revolt against the weekly washday is clear from the middle-class budgets already quoted, for it was becoming a recognised thing that the washing might be " put out " ; but this was only possible for a limited section even of town dwellers. In most middle-class homes in country and suburb, all the washing was done at home, right to the end of the century, and even up to the Great War. Most white articles were starched, and every competent housewife and maidservant could starch and iron the men's shirts and collars and cuffs, and goffer those elaborate, stiff, and uncomfortable frills which adorned the maid's cap and the baby's bonnet, the two year old's frock and mamma's chemise. Percy Lubbock, in *Earlham*, feelingly describes his childhood hostility towards the clean " starched and crackling tissues " in which he had to clothe himself on Sundays.

Those two great aids to the present simplification of housework, gas and electricity, scarcely affected the issue. Gas lighting was in fairly wide use in towns by 1870, the " bat's wing " or luminous flat flame being the source of light ; but where a householder was advanced enough to have gas installed, it was commonly found only in the downstairs rooms, candles being used in the bed-rooms. Reception rooms were usually lit by petroleum oil lamps, most of which were dangerous if carelessly handled. In 1883 the first company for the distribution of electricity for lighting purposes was formed. Carbon filament lamps were the first source of domestic electric light—the metal filament lamps now commonly used were not perfected until the end of the century. The danger of competition, however, woke up the gas industry, which, though established in 1813, had made very little effort to improve the quality of its product or the methods of gas consumption. The incandescent mantle, invented in 1885, was not brought to a sufficient pitch of perfection and cheapness for commercial exploitation until 1893. Within a few years from that date, it was in general use for gas lighting, and had been applied also to the oil lamp. Domestic artificial lighting, for the first time in the history of mankind, was at last within sight of adequacy. The next great invention in gas lighting, the inverted burner, belongs to the opening years of the new century.

The impetus given by the spectre of electric competition had other important results for domestic life. Thomas Fletcher, after studying the possibilities of the Bunsen burner, invented in 1855, adapted the principle to heating appliances, and from 1890 onwards various types of domestic fires were produced. These did not become popular until after 1907, largely owing to the original failure of manufacturers to realise the necessity of fitting adequate flues. The gas cooker was almost unknown in England until 1907, though it was in use on the Continent some years earlier.

Cooking was done on immense kitchen ranges which swallowed coal by the bucket (a fact of less moment in those days than it would be to-day, since coal averaged less than £1 a ton). These domestic engines were often temperamental : if the wind set in a particular direction, the fire would not draw or the oven would not heat. They were agreeable enough kitchen companions in the winter, but in summer they made cooking a torture. Jams, preserves, and pickles were made at home, in the stillroom if the house boasted one, in the kitchen if not. In winter, much coal carrying was involved by the open fires in all living-rooms, which had to be laid, lighted, and replenished during the day. Fortunately for the domestic staff, fires in the bedroom were a luxury allowed only during illness except in rich households.

Multitudinous " brights "—brass and steel fenders, fire-irons, and ornaments ; copper pans and dish-covers ; silver teapots, dishes, cruets, and toast racks, as well as table silver—all had to be kept clean and polished. Stainless knives were unknown, and knife-cleaning machines suspect. Carpets were hand swept, furniture and knick-knacks hand dusted. French polish was despised— elbow grease was considered as effective, and far more virtuous. In fact, the work of even a moderate sized house involved a vast amount of hard manual labour. Servants were expected to work willingly all round the clock, and to accept in return low wages, poor food (it was the exception for domestics, even in small households, to eat the same food as the family), and dark, comfortless sleeping quarters.

Most housewives refused to acknowledge the restiveness of the domestic servant as something more than a passing phase. They would not see that it was a definite new element in the organisation of home life which must be accepted and countered with reforms in the conditions under which domestics lived and worked, and with the elimination of all unnecessary labour. Labour saving inventions were continually being applied in industry during the nineteenth century ; but not until the twentieth were they adapted for use in the home. Employers grumbled to one another about the inefficiency and unwillingness of the modern servant, some wrote letters to the papers, and all but a few endeavoured to carry on life as they felt it ought to be. Those few were the pioneers of twentieth century domesticity. In an article published in the *Examiner* during the late 'seventies, a strong plea is made for some form of co-operative housekeeping :

" To give up home would be too great a sacrifice to be repaid by any amount of comfort and freedom from cares. . . . But if domestic life cannot be made enjoyable without the sacrifice of that appearance of isolation which to many people represents a home it would surely be wise to yield the appearance for the reality, to seem to have no home for the sake of having a true one—that is, a place for happiness and rest. . . . If expenditure of money, of time, and of health, on the mere brute necessaries of existence can by any method of co-operative

"MY FIRST DINNER PARTY: At Grace's you get the prettiest table decorations, the dullest conversation, and (I'm told) the best dinners in London. It was a rather a pretty idea to have Neapolitan violets floating in all the finger-glasses. Several people got quite brisk as they picked them out and made dear little bouquets. A middle-aged M.P. took me in, and seemed to think me a great bore!" (From a Debutante's Diary, 1890)

supply be lessened without loss of those necessaries and with gain of higher employments, will our leg of mutton taste the worse ? "

The writer goes on to advocate the recently introduced flat system as a solution of housekeeping difficulties. She enumerates the objections—that tradesmen's messengers look on a block of flats as one address ; that rents are enormous in proportion to house rents ; that the post office refuses to do more than leave letters in the street hall. Too frequently there is a deficiency of the needful offices : " Peabody's trustees appear to have larger views of the scullery work and storage needs of household life in their workmen's homes than do most of the builders of these high-rented flats, where well-to-do people are meant to live in well-to-do style and to give dinners and crushes to well-to-do friends." Lifts, " which ought to be looked on as a necessary," both for persons and goods, are beginning to be recognised by shrewd landlords as a needful addition to staircases if their flats are to increase in popularity. Finally, " attempts have been made to provide the home privacy of the flat combined with the freedom from household cares of the hotel. You have your own dwelling, your own furniture, but not your own servants : your concern with your meals is to order them, to eat them, and to pay for them, and you have the privilege of finding fault with them without setting your Lucilla's cap awry. . . . In some of the mansions which thus offer us in our homes the ' world's best welcome ' of an inn, if not in all, public rooms to be used at will complete the arrangements and afford something like the combined independence of a club. . . . If the attendance can be kept well-regulated and ample there seems no reason why this sort of home-hotel or co-operative home should not be altogether successful."

Service flats in the days of Queen Victoria !

" When the Thompsons invite, on a Christmas Night, their bachelor cousin—meaning me,
They expect his aid at the grand parade of their charming and numerous progeny " (*Graphic Christmas Number*, 1871)

" YOUNG DECORUM : At a juvenile ball the children cannot, of course, be left to themselves. If they were, all these pretty, well-ordered things would soon be romping on the floor, tearing one another's hair and dresses, exchanging slaps and pinches, complaints and defiances, and generally doing things in which it should be reserved for dogs to delight. Entertainments of this kind are part of social education " (1870)

"WITCHCRAFT IN THE HOME : Rendered curious by the recent spiritualistic recordings of ladies being conveyed through the air, Mr. Walter Thornbury, the well-known *littérateur*, paid half a crown for admission to a séance in Hamburg Square. Two professional mediums requested the visitors to join hands, and the gas was turned down. One sceptic was struck on the head by a speaking-trumpet, sofa cushions and an antimacassar were flung at another. But Mr. Thornbury left in a hardened state of unbelief" (1871)

" Oh! we've all been shopping, shop, shop, shopping, we've visited the Lowther, and the Burlington Arcade;
And we're all of us a dropping, drop, drop, dropping fast asleep, except papa, that idle man, who only paid "
(*Graphic Christmas Number*, 1876)

" EAST OR WEST, HOME'S BEST : This Morning Room shows how an ingle nook can be added to any ordinary-sized room. The spaces on the outside are adapted for bookshelves, and the lower part to the cupboards so dear to English housewives. Brilliantly coloured Burmantofts ware should adorn the shelves. The curtains and covers are of plain plush. The mantelshelf is convenient for a panel-announcement 'East or West, Home's Best.' The window-recess, with ottoman, is another cosy feature " (1889)

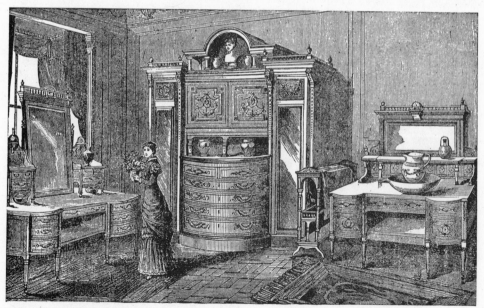

" FOR THE BEST BEDROOM : A suite of furniture in cream with pink decorations designed by a leading London house and exhibited in the Suffolk Street Galleries " (1882)

ROYAL APARTMENTS (1): "H.M.'s Sitting Room at Osborne House, Isle of Wight" (1880)

ROYAL APARTMENTS (2): "The Drawing Room at Balmoral is draped in Balmoral tartan—a quaint, warm, grey design, arranged by the late Prince Consort. It is far superior in design and colour to the startling and gaudy Royal Stuart tartan" (1882)

"MY FIRST BALL: I was taken down to supper by a man who didn't pay me a single compliment. At first he talked to me exactly as if I were not grown up, but afterwards I was surprised to find how much I knew about books and that kind of thing; but then, one is never appreciated at home"
(From a Debutante's Diary, 1890)

" THE SUPREME MOMENT : The bride is ready for church. It seems a shame to put on the veil which, for a time, will hide her charms from the man of her heart. In the background, Mamma and the governess regard with loving admiration their favourite, so soon to be taken from them " (1890)

" STEP-DANCING IN SOCIETY : A *pas de quatre* in the drawing-room has come to be welcomed.
The average young man is showing a disinclination for ball-rooms, and it seems difficult to find
enough of him. There is thus a growing popularity of step dancing by young ladies " (1892)

"CREATING AN IMPRESSION—THE NEW GOVERNESS ARRIVES" (1892)

"AGRICULTURAL FAMILIES AT HOME: Insufficient sleeping accommodation, defective ventilation, paucity of light, and almost utter absence of drainage render the labourer's cottage a source of demoralisation against which the influence of the clergyman cannot contend. Our illustration shows the ordinary dwelling of a Northamptonshire labourer. His daughter wears one of those pink cotton hoods, so useful for preventing the faces of labouring girls from tan by the sun. The labourer's wife is busily engaged in suckling her infant. As for the children, their toys will soon be ruthlessly put away preparatory to the ablutions associated with the close of the week" (1872)

III

DOWN AMONG THE MASSES

DISRAELI'S division of England into two nations was as true of the last half of Victoria's reign as of the first, and even truer of the feminine half of the population than of the masculine. Apart from domestic servants, the women of the masses scarcely existed for the ladies of the classes. Some of them, particularly the wives of estate workers and agricultural labourers, contrived to be clean and tidy enough to be worthy of charitable notice ; but the majority—the factory workers, sweated out-workers, and working-men's wives of the towns—lived out of sight (and out of mind) in streets and districts where the lady never penetrated. If by some curious oversight she strayed into a slum-quarter, where one room served a family for all the purposes of living, she elevated her nose, and fled from the venomous stench emanating from these " homes." She wondered how " those creatures " could live in such squalor : she did not pause to reflect on their lack of choice in the matter. A respectable working-class quarter was, to outward seeming, hardly better, for most of the women, clean though they kept their thriftily furnished homes, were too tired with the struggle to make ends meet to be other than slovens in their persons. Unwashed and uncombed, their clothes pinned together for want of a few stitches, they went about their household duties and exchanged morning greetings with their neighbours.

The Victorian lady saw no social moral in such a contrast as that depicted in the pictures called " Valentine Makers and Receivers," reproduced on page 94. She merely felt a little sentimentally that the custom of sending valentines was really a good thing, since they were pleasant to receive and supplied agreeable work for the nimble fingers of the amorphous poor. That the work was niggling and therefore exhausting never crossed her mind ; and that the women who made these charming souvenirs received but a few pence an hour for the joint labour of themselves and their children was a fact outside her cognisance.

The workers in her home she knew at close range, and she did not approve of them. She found them untruthful, lazy, indifferent. They were of another clay than herself. Consequently they did not need such good food as she, or so much of it. Attics with low pitched ceilings and no fireplaces, which were freezing cold in winter and broiling hot in summer, served them for bedrooms, and dark dank basements which never saw daylight were good enough for their living quarters. In the London houses belonging to some of our poorer peers, the dismal conditions in which all town domestics passed their existence in the Victorian era can still be studied.

And when one of these unfriended young creatures allowed herself to be seduced into sexual love, with its almost inevitable Consequence, she had no hope of either understanding or mercy from her employer. An indignant housewife of the 'sixties, writing to a ladies' newspaper on the prevalent immoral conduct of neighbours in filching servants from one another by promises of better wages and conditions, relates her own experiences. One new maid was persuaded to change her situation by a nearby doctor : " When her month was up, she left me. . . . A Nemesis attended on the deed as a matter of course, for the doctor had to turn her out of the house, as the phrase goes, ' neck and crop ' at a moment's notice. Not a fortnight ago I lost another servant whom two of my neighbours had been tampering with. . . . In this case also a Nemesis was at hand, and the best of the joke was, that after I had turned her adrift, the lady who had been most anxious for her wouldn't have her at any price." . . . Such extreme callousness towards a fellow creature would be incredible were it not so blatantly recorded.

Wretched as were the living conditions of the workers in the industrial areas, they were less brutalising than those in the slum areas of big cities. If there were no personal privacy, there was at least family privacy. A German miner who spent some years of his working life in Northumberland wrote a record of his experiences for the information of his fellow miners in Germany. The account has a special interest because it is that of a man who approached the life he described from the inside, whereas most recorders of workers' conditions write from the outside. His standards are those of the working man, not of the middle-class social reformer ; and according to those standards he found life in England far more comfortable than in Germany. He comments with surprise on the spirit of comradeship in the pits—comradeship born of life lived in common and constant peril—which caused the young and strong to allot to the old and maimed the less dangerous and difficult workings, and made both workman and official forget differences of status in face of the tragic emergencies of the pit.

The miners lived in houses built on two floors for two families, each floor with a number and a separate front door, and comprising a front bedroom twelve feet by fifteen, and a back living-room fifteen feet square, also slept in " if the family is a large one." In the small projecting kitchen-scullery at the back, nine feet by seven and a half, with a little window and a big copper, the miner's wife rid her man's clothes of the dirt of the pits : " The dirty linen is steeped in cold water overnight, wrung out next morning, flung into a copper, soap and soda thrown in, and boiling water added. Then it is thumped for ten minutes with a mallet weighing six or seven pounds. . . . The linen is then taken out, brushed, again boiled and thumped, and then it is clean. If the mallet is too heavy, a steel spring a foot long is tied with a string to the ceiling, and the mallet attached to it. Then one has only to press downwards, the mallet flies up of itself."

Each double house had a backyard eighteen feet square with a coal store for each tenant, and a closet common to both. " There are no garrets and there is no cellar, so that nothing can be stored. This is the one thing wanting in these dwellings," concludes the German recorder. The rent of the lower flat was five shillings and sixpence, of the upper five shillings a week. In some streets, the windows projected, and each flat was provided with a bathroom, at an extra rental of sixpence or a shilling.

Many miners' wives ordered their provisions in bulk from shops doing a large trade. A few days before pay-day, the tradesman called for orders, and an hour after pay-time the laden carts drew up outside the miners' houses, the goods were received, and the accounts settled on the spot. The cost of the principal items of working-class food fluctuated very little during the last thirty years of the century. Wheaten flour cost from 10*d*. to 1*s*. 6*d*. a stone, bread 7*d*. a quartern, beef from 3½*d*. to 9½*d*. a pound, mutton from 4*d*. to 6*d*. a pound, block salt ¼*d*., rice 1½*d*. to 2½*d*., fine sugar 1*d*. to 1½*d*., loaf sugar 2*d*., currants 1½*d*. to 2½*d*., butter 1*s*. to 1*s*. 4*d*., margarine 5*d*. to 11*d*., Dutch cheese 5¼*d*., bar soap 1½*d*. to 2½*d*. Tea, which in the 'seventies cost from 5*s*. to 10*s*. the pound and was therefore out of reach of the working class, by the 'nineties could be had for 1*s*. to 1*s*. 6*d*., and was an important item in their consumption.

The relative cheapness of meat meant that the wife of a skilled worker could provide him with bacon and eggs for breakfast, bread and cheese or meat to take with him to work, a meal of meat and pudding or soup and meat when he came home, and a supper of bread and cheese or meat. She herself and the rest of the family fared more meagrely, until the children were old enough to add to the household income, which was soon enough : they were allowed to begin work as half-timers at ten (in 1891 the age was raised to eleven). At thirteen they became full-timers, provided they had attained a certain standard of school proficiency. The Mines Regulation Act of 1860, which forbade women to work underground in mines, allowed boys to go underground at twelve.

By the 'nineties the average wage for a man in industry had risen to £1 a week. Skilled workers in some industries earned half as much again. Wages were highest in the booming cotton trade—a mule spinner could make about 35*s*. a week. A miner working a good seam in a good mine could earn 30*s*. A puddler earned 30*s*., his assistant 21*s*. A policeman began at 21*s*. and rose to 30*s*. The average wage of the agricultural worker, on the other hand, was 12*s*. On such sums the wives of working men were expected to rear families of six, seven, eight—a dozen.

The death rate among their children was appalling, and the market for unskilled and casual work was saturated with undersized beings half starved from birth. The evidence available tends to show that, hard as was their lot, the children of working men whose wives did not themselves go out to work stood a better chance of survival than those of couples who both worked. In the Registrar-General's report for 1891, the death rate for children under five at Portsmouth was given as 59.4 per thousand, London 78.6, Newcastle 73.2, while in Salford, in the cotton area, it was 93.8, in Birmingham 95.2, and in Sheffield 95.9.

The prohibition of the employment of mothers, at least until all their children were past the age of three, was a favourite plan among social reformers. Heartrending pictures were drawn of children sent supperless to bed and husband arriving home to a cold hearth and no food because his wife, worn out by her early morning domestic labours and her day's work in mill or factory, had retired to rest too exhausted to attend to his creature comforts. The over-worked wife-mother-partial-breadwinner deserved some of the sympathy heaped upon her husband's head. A system of shared domestic as well as factory labour would have lightened the bleakness of a hard existence and doubled the value of the wife's additional earnings.

Town infants who survived must have been tough, for their mothers were in the habit of leaving them in the charge of a " minder " as ignorant as them-selves, and in addition quite indifferent to the welfare of the babies by whose care she made her own meagre living. Their cries of pain or hunger—for some, especially the illegitimate, were deliberately starved—were stilled with a death dealing concoction known as Godfrey's Cordial, a compound of opium, treacle, and an infusion of sassafras.[1] The results of the maltreatment of the infants of working mothers are shown in the report already quoted, for " in the first week of life, the town rate exceeds the rural rate by 23%, in the second week by 64%, in the third week by 83%, and in the fourth week by 97%. In the first month the town mortality is 27% above the rural rate, in the second month 121% above it, and the excess goes on increasing until in the sixth month it amounts to no less than 273%. This is the month in which the difference is greatest, though it remains throughout the rest of the year at a not very much lower point." Illegitimate infants stood the worst chance, for it was accepted that So-and-So's third or fourth " little unwanted " should follow its predecessors to an early grave.

The average wage earned by working women at this period was 10s. a week, and the woman alone naturally shirked the impossible task of supporting her infants. On this sum, in the opinion of inquirers of the day, a girl living by herself could manage to keep herself " respectable." On less, the girl living at home and paying 4s. or 5s. a week for board was said to be content ; but for the girl maintaining herself the struggle was rarely successful—she eked out her wretched pay by irregular prostitution. The cheap lodging houses for couples known as " the doubles " were little more than low class brothels. Even married women, in bad times, sometimes solicited, especially when under the influence of drink : for women as well as men were ready enough to drown their miseries in alcohol, no difficult matter when beer was 1d., and whisky 3s. a pint. Tipsy women were as plentiful in the streets as tipsy men when closing time came on Saturday nights.

The best paid women, like the best paid men, were those employed in the cotton industry. A weaver could earn 24s. a week all the year round. The ring and throstle (women) spinners, however, rarely earned more than 14s. or 15s. Warpers and women in the cardroom earned from 18s. to 20s., winders slightly less. In the woollen industry, where men and women worked at the same processes and wages in general were lower, women were victims of

---

[1] Such " Godfrey's Cordial " as may still occasionally be dispensed is devoid of opium, and therefore innocuous.

" A STREET BALL: Everybody who has perambulated humble streets in the metropolis has witnessed the scene in our engraving. On a summer evening we have seen a hundred couples moving to the organ-grinder's tunes. The girls are generally better behaved than the boys, who are apt to introduce an offensively Ethiopian element " (1872

" EMIGRANTS FEEDING : Most emigrants who cross the Atlantic nowadays are carried in steamships, which perform the trip in from ten to seventeen days, instead of the six weeks for sail. The food supplied to emigrants bound for Dame Columbia is plentiful in quantity and not deficient in quality, but the cooking is often very repulsive to poor creatures with squeamish stomachs. Our picture shows the scene between decks at dinner time. One steward is serving out soup, another is delivering portions of boiled meat " (1872)

consistently reduced payment, even for piece work, simply because they were women. In Huddersfield, for instance, the deductions on piece work varied from 15 to 30 per cent. for various types of goods on looms running 50 picks a minute ; on looms running 70–80 picks a minute, the women received only half the men's wages, with proportionate deductions for piecework ; on looms running 110–120 picks a minute, they received only a third. These arbitrary deductions were made despite the fact that they were as skilful and quick as the men. At Bradford, women wool-combers earned 12s., against the men's 18s. Many Yorkshire weavers' earnings were no more than 8s. or 9s. a week, and at the best rarely rose above 18s. In a carpet mill at Halifax, women's wages averaged 13s. 9d. a week, men's £1 1s. 8d. for the same work.

The linen workers of Belfast, whose long hours of labour were carried on in such unhealthy conditions that their average working life was under twenty years (those who remained in the factories more than a few years died in their twenties or thirties of consumption) were paid 8s. to 9s. a week. The silk throwsters of Macclesfield averaged throughout the year 6s. a week, though their trade was semi-seasonal and during the good season women at the power looms earned 12s. a week. The crape in which Victorian ladies mourned so lavishly was made by women paid at the rate of 5s. a week. In the French polishing and printing trades women averaged 9s. or 10s. a week, men two or three times as much. Tin plate, ironworks, and brickworks women operatives received 7s. 6d. a week ; white lead workers 2s. a day. In the nail-making trade in 1883 women's wages were 3s. to 5s. a week. A hosiery seamer could make 11s. to 16s. in the factory ; 2s. 6d. to 3s. (per week !) if she were an out-worker. Skilled cigar makers sometimes earned as much as 30s. a week, though the average wage for women in the tobacco trade was 6s. or 7s.

Confectioners began at 3s. 6d. a week and rose to 8s. Button makers' earnings varied between 10s. and 15s., dressmakers' and milliners' between 10s. and £1 a week. Tailoresses, working in a workshop from 7 a.m. to 7 p.m., earned 12s. a week ; for a waistcoat made at home in six hours, they received 1s. 6d., and many of them were only too ready to take home such work in order to add a little to their workshop pittance. Laundresses, whose work was both dangerous, on account of unprotected machinery, and unhealthy, and whose hours were unlimited, earned for washing 2s. 6d. to 2s. 11d. a day, for ironing 3s. to 3s. 6d. a day.

One little group of middle class reformers recommended that ladies should set up provident clubs for working girls : " the women are thus protected from being forced from misfortune to take very low wages, while, on the other hand, they are preserved from being compelled to ask absurdly high ones."

A certain Mr. Roebuck asserted in 1844, when it was first proposed to limit the hours worked by women, that, " labour in factories is . . . warm and comfortable. . . . Medical men declare that women in factories . . . are a far better race for the propagation of the species than any other class of labourer." He knew little of the inside of factories, for they were certainly worse in 1844 than they were thirty years later. Factories had been built exclusively with a view to creating the best conditions for the article to be manufactured. The needs of the wretches who must, in spite of machinery's rapid advances, be employed in them received scarcely a moment's thought. Sanitary arrangements were grossly defective, and in some cases non-existent. Provision for ventilation was the exception. In the cotton weaving sheds, the normal temperature was 90°, and steam jets were placed within a few inches of the workers' heads. The sudden change from the damp, hot atmosphere inside the factory to the cold outer air led to the general development of consumption and other lung complaints among the workers. Rheumatism was common. Conditions in the linen weaving sheds of Belfast were similar.

In many of the places where the nailmakers earned their miserable wages, they depended, even in the daytime, on the furnaces for much of their light. After dark, their only light was from the forge and the hot iron. The phosphorus used in the making of lucifer matches gave rise to a particularly horrible disease, necrosis of the jaw, which, first attacking the jawbone, worked its way through teeth and gums. Workers in the white lead mills inevitably fell victims to the poisonous fumes of the dangerous material they handled : at first it brought on faintness, sickness, and weakness ; but if in spite of these physical warnings the worker persisted, she was bound for death, by way of colic, epilepsy, paralysis, blindness, madness. The commonest manifestation of the more advanced stage of white-lead poisoning was a form of paralysis known as " wrist-drop " which rendered the wrist powerless. The women in white lead works carried the poisonous stuff back and forth and up and down ladders on their heads—toil so burdensome that men refused to do it.

Women suffered a great deal from the bullying of the " overlookers," who were prone to expect, and, if their expectations went unfulfilled, to exact, sexual intercourse from their underlings. (Is it to be wondered that the unloved offspring of such unions were left to starve, or to the more merciful end of drugging with Godfrey's Cordial ?)

The system of fines was comprehensive. For being late, a penny was deducted for the first five minutes, up to 3d. and 6d. according to the time lost. For being found in the wrong shed, for laughing, for sitting down, the fines ranged from 6d. to 2s. 6d. Flaws in weaving met the ultimatum that the weaver at fault must either buy the piece or submit to a heavy fine. In some factories, the worker found herself mulcted of a large proportion of her earnings for flaws alleged to have been found in her work, but was not allowed to see the allegedly faulty piece. Deductions from wages were also sometimes made for the use of hot water, for the oiling of the looms, for the renewal and repair of brushes and oil cans, and for the cleaning of the lavatories.

" A SALVATION ARMY SHELTER : A hush pervades the hall of the women's shelter in Whitechapel, wherein the destitute sit till bed-time. Pinched, white, forlorn faces defiantly regard unwelcome intruders upon their misery. Late comers, finding the place full, beg very hard to lie on the forms in the hall until morning. Those who can afford it have the luxury of a penny supper, after which they wait for prayers, some of them stitching at torn corners of their scanty raiment. Over the supports of the upper dormitory or gallery, is the awful question, in red and white, ' ARE YOU READY TO DIE ?' When the night is still, half the inmates look as though they were dead already ; the unsightly receptacles for the sleepers are strangely like open coffins ". (1892)

More than one battle for reduced hours was fought by the men from " behind the women's petticoats," for Victoria's parliaments could often be induced to a sentimental solicitude for the woes of overworked women and children when the miseries of the overworked adult male left them cold. It had been found that in practice a shorter working day for women and children, who were for the most part engaged in different processes from the men, led to a shorter working day for men. The middle class champions of women were blind to this aspect of restrictive legislation relating to women's hours of employment. In a collective work on the conditions of working women, the authors state that " to pretend that women wish to have their hours of work restricted by legislation is not honest." This statement was no doubt true of the sweated out-workers, and of the lowest paid unorganised factory workers who feared to lose their ill-paid drudgery altogether if difficulties were put in the way of their working themselves blind and mad to propitiate their callous employers. But where men and women were organised in the same trade unions, the women were as alive to the actual situation as the men.

Women had been included in 1844 in the restriction to 12 hours a day already imposed on young persons of thirteen to eighteen ; and in 1850 work in textile factories was further limited to 12 hours less 1½ hours for meal-times on the first five working days of the week and to 7½ hours on Saturdays. In 1874 half an hour was taken off each of the first five days, and 1 hour off Saturday, making a total of 56½ working hours per week. By 1878 there was a legal maximum of 60 hours a week.

The Factory Act of 1891 abolished overtime in textile factories, but allowed women to put in 2 hours a night on 48 evenings of the year in so-called seasonal trades (bookbinding and the making of wearing apparel among their number), and in trades subject to weather conditions. In the fruit and fish preserving trade, and in the making of condensed milk, women were permitted by law to work for 14 hours a day, less mealtimes, for 96 days during any one year. In 1895 the number of evenings per year was reduced to 30, with a maximum of three in any one week. Laundering was the one trade in which night work by women was still allowed.

Contrary to the opinions expressed by those against the limitation of hours, more and more women came to be employed in industry as the hours of work were shortened : in 1841, just under half a million worked in factories, in 1891 just under a million and a half. Such amelioration as crept into their lives by the end of the century was due in very small measure to concerted efforts by themselves on their own behalf. It came through the demands of the men's trade unions, and through the gradual opening of the eyes of some members of the privileged classes to the disgraces of the industrial system. But though women's trade unionism belongs to the twentieth century, it had its faint beginnings in the nineteenth when in 1874 the Women's Protective and Provident League, afterwards re-christened the Women's Trade Union League, was founded. Women were admitted to the Trades Union Congress in 1875, and each year thereafter saw the formation of new groups of women workers, some of which proved ephemeral while others weathered the stormy passage between internal dissension and external pressure. Only once was the popular imagination struck by women's trade union activities, and that was in 1888 when, after the publication of a fiery article by Mrs. Annie Besant describing the awful conditions of the match-makers' trade, 672 girls employed in an East London factory came out on strike. They had no funds and no organisation, and the struggle would have been hopeless but for Mrs. Besant and Herbert Burrows, who succeeded in rousing opinion in support of the strikers. A public subscription was opened, and brought in £400; and after a fortnight the match girls' employers were compelled, by pressure of popular feeling, to give way. The girls went back to their jobs with a union nearly a thousand strong.

The fate of the shop assistant was no better than that of the factory hand. By the 'nineties, something like four-fifths of the workers in the drapery trade were women. Their hours of work varied from 90 per week in Chelsea, Fulham and Hammersmith to 63½ in Holloway; from 66–68 in the centre of Manchester to 80 in the suburbs of that city. In working class districts the shops were kept open very late on Saturdays. The average wage of women shop assistants was about 10s. a week, and their lives were governed by an extensive system of fines. An assistant leaving her post on account of illness was in many houses fined for absence. If she failed to make a sale, even when the article required was not in stock, she was sometimes fined. In one large London house, an assistant was fined 6d. for standing on a chair; for sending bad money to the cashier, she had to make up the deficiency and pay 1s. fine; for omitting to credit premiums on the exchange or return of goods once 2s. 6d. fine, for the same offence a second time, dismissal; and so on through a hundred petty offences.

Living in was the general rule, and the value of the board and lodging supplied was usually assessed at £40 a year; though when, as sometimes happened after long years of service, an assistant gained the privilege of living out, not more than £20 a year would be added to her wage. In some firms, food was adequate and living accommodation decent. In too many, the reverse was the case. It was no unusual thing for assistants to be locked out of the living-in houses on Sundays and left without food. Those who had friends to visit possibly found this no great hardship; how the others passed their day of rest, since neither cheap eating houses nor cheap places of entertainment were open on Sundays, it is impossible to conceive.

"THE LOST CHILD : There is something ludicrously hopeless in the thought that the lost little female urchin, who has drifted from Paradise Court, may belong to any of the three million inhabitants of our modern Babylon. A huge friendly giant of a policeman has swooped down, and asked her with kind roughness where she comes from. A boy screaming *Echo ! third edition !* stops to see ' what's up with the kid.' With one faint scream of joy and frenzy, the mother suddenly breaks through the crowd, and, careless of bystanders, she clasps to her aching heart the sobbing, dishevelled, frightened little Elsie. The angels who led the mother to her child look down and smile with love and pity " (1870)

"RAG FAIR, MANCHESTER : In the Rag Fair threadbare garments, translated by cunning hands into a delusive freshness, are sold to the needy poor of Manchester. A factory girl has come to buy a dress. She holds it against herself, to see how it will fit" (1870)

" THE SUNDAY DINNER: The bakers' premises at 1 p.m. on Sunday present an animated prospect, and as you pass them after Church your appetite is sharpened by brown or yellow dishes containing nicely browned potatoes and a steaming batter pudding " (1873)

MRS. FOGGINS ON MEAT: " Taking advantage of the high price of butcher's meat, an ex-Australian colonist appeared in Newcastle and persuaded the wives of working men to try the new preserved meat from the Antipodes. He gave an Australian banquet in the Assembly Rooms, where enthusiasm reached its height when Mrs. Foggins, spoon in hand, rose to return thanks from the women of Newcastle and Gateshead " (1872)

"IDYLL IN GOLDEN SQUARE: Here is one of those poetic incidents of London street-life which Thackeray loved to contemplate. The love passage between blue-frocked knight of the cleaver and pretty perambulator-guider is happily situated, for this Square with the auriferous title and the air of decayed gentility belongs to poetry" (1870)

"VALENTINE MAKERS AND RECEIVERS : The manufacture of the more tasteful valentines furnishes remunerative employment to many young women and children. Valentine makers, as a class, are clean, obedient and skilful. There is no prettier sight than that of light, nimble fingers swiftly evolving grace and order out of a chaos of lace paper, artificial flowers, little pictures, mottoes, and bits of ribbon" (1875)

" A LOW LODGING-HOUSE : The common lodging-houses in St. Giles's present singular studies of misfortune, folly and crime. While some of the women are clean, honest and sober, others are addicted to drunkenness and gross vice. For *3d.* and *4d.* a night one may find bed, warm fire, cooking appliances and congenial company. A house may produce a clear profit of three or four hundred pounds a year. Four common lodging-houses in St. Giles's mean a neat brougham and a suburban villa " (1872)

"AN ANIMALS' PUBLIC HOUSE : The Drinking Fountains Association has provided troughs for horses and cattle, and small reservoirs on a lower level for the use of dogs. The drayhorses and poor old cab-horses are staunch teetotallers who scorn to drown their sorrows in alcohol, and thereby set a good example to the beer-and-gin-imbibing Jehus who drive them ". (1876)

"POVERTY'S BREATHING SPACE: Much of the surplus poverty of the towns finds its way once a year to the hop plantations, there to earn a little money, breathe some fresh air, and enjoy a taste of country life. It sleeps where it can, in barns and outhouses or under hedges, and does its own cooking, when there is anything to cook" (1876)

" SACK-MAKING IN THE EAST END : In a court leading from a squalid street off Ratcliffe Highway, our artist came on a small band of women below the street lamp. An order for a certain number of sacks had come in late at night. The work had to be done by the morning, and the workers were gathered round the lamp to save their oil or candle " (1875)

" THE JUBILEE MUG : The feeling on the occasion of the Queen's Jubilee was most touchingly evidenced by scenes such as this. Away in dingy side-streets poor folk lit with candles their narrow window-spaces. If the Queen had seen this it would doubtless have affected her as the widow's offering affected a Higher Personality " (1887)

" RESCUED COLLIERS : Ten days after the Troedyhriw pit-flooding, a rescuer cut his way through. He was touched by a grimy hand ; then arms were flung around his neck, and he felt himself kissed fervently. The 14 missing colliers were brought out and fed, wrapped in blankets, and taken to hospital, where hot bricks were placed to their feet. Above are a pitman and family " (1877)

"CHILDREN IN THE TEMPLE GARDENS: The opening of Inner Temple Gardens on summer evenings is a great boon for artisans' children in the densely peopled regions round the Temple. Parents, after their work, have leisure to tidy their children for an outing" (1883)

"A TROOPERS' BALL: Participants of the ball given by troopers of the Second Life Guards in St. James's Hall included enlisted men from other regiments, as well as several good-humoured officers. The variety of uniforms made a pretty sight" (1884)

" THE WIDOW'S CHAIR : When pensions and half-pay are collected, the Bluejacket's widow sits with her children, receiving small sums cheerfully given by men drawing money. Ten pounds is as much as she can hope for, but this, with the year's pay at times granted by the Admiralty, is all that the widow has for facing the world " (1892)

" A LODGING-HOUSE KITCHEN : The charge for a bed in this Spitalfields common lodging-house is fourpence, ' doubles ' being eightpence. The bedclothes are boldly marked ' Stolen,' but this does not prevent the feminine lodger from making them into under-clothing during the night. The kitchen forms the club-room, where each lodger cooks his or her provisions " (1886)

MORAL PIT-BROW WOMEN : " Underground working by women has been forbidden, but their employment at the pit's mouth is healthier than factory labour, and the girls are both moral and well conducted. This dress, designed by Mrs. Blundell, gives freedom to every limb " (1886)

"BANK HOLIDAY: All are 'on pleasure bent.' The cyclist is present in great force—the energy which the knights of the wheel display on the hottest of hot days is inexplicable to those who are not cyclists, and prefer to lounge slowly along, or to enjoy the *dolce far niente* by basking in the sun, like the parent on the left of the picture" (1890)

IV

INTO THE OPEN

LIFE in the country in the nineteenth century was as calm and settled as it had been in the eighteenth. The coming of the railway had made transport quicker, but it had not affected the accepted yearly cycle of the landed proprietor, who would no more have thought of spending his summers sun-bathing in California and his winters sun-bathing in South Africa than he would have thought of flying to Paris for the day. To please his wife and daughters, he spent the spring in London, but August found him back at his country home for the shooting or the fishing, to be followed in due season by the cubbing and the hunting.

A man of wealth did not deny himself the indulgence of his whims. If he felt that the grounds round his mansion would be improved by the addition of some century-old oaks, he gave orders that a few should be removed from their woodland birthplaces to the positions he desired to adorn. Or if he had a fancy to fish trout and had no suitable stream near by, he thought nothing of employing a hundred villagers for months in dredging a lake so that he could indulge in his favourite sport for a matter of three summer weeks.

Woman's part in manly sports was largely confined to that of admiring onlooker. It was exceptional for a woman to handle a gun, even in the 'nineties when many freedoms had been won. Women rode to hounds long before 1870, and did so increasingly; but their daring did not meet with anything like universal approval. Unsuitable clothes, and the reputation for feminine delicacy which most of them endeavoured to maintain, debarred all but those at the hobbledehoy stage from taking serious part in otter hunting and beagling. Tight corsets and skirts that sweep the ground are not adapted to physical activity. Gladstone's third daughter, Mary (afterwards Mrs. Drew), who enjoyed a good deal more freedom and activity than most of her contemporaries, wrote in her diary on October 23, 1877, " Went up the Lesser Sugar Loaf, steepest bit at the top not made easier by a tremendous wind which, getting inside my gown, nearly carried me away." Only intrepid young women dared thus to face the possibility of involuntary ballooning.

No less daring were the hunting girls of the period who, clad in flowing skirts and a tall hat, and riding side-saddle, took their fences as boldly as did the men; and if reckless riding landed them in an unexpected ditch, under instead of on their mounts, they took their falls as bravely as their fences— and often thanked heaven for the tall hat which had saved them from a broken crown.

Girls fortunate enough to have homes favourably situated learned to fish for trout. Lady Colin Campbell, an enthusiastic fisherwoman, enjoyed nothing better than to set out alone for some favourite spot on a familiar Highland stream. " A companion is a useless incumbrance to the true worshipper of the noble art of trout-fishing," she declared. Armed with a little flask of whisky against the dangers of a chill, and carrying " fishing basket, landing-net, small eight-ounce rod of split cane, and a little pocket-book of different coloured midges," she rarely returned empty handed. She liked to dress for her fishing expeditions " in a pair of tweed knickerbockers, kilt skirt, loose, many-pocketed coat, woollen stockings, and thick hob-nailed shoes, out of which the water can squelch as easily as it enters," though a rival fisherwoman of the same era recommends instead of shoes very thick boots well greased to keep out the wet.

Women bold enough to go out with the guns were rare. Shooting parties were, indeed, episodes of almost unrelieved boredom for the ladies. After a more than usually substantial breakfast—were they not about to revert to the status of primitive hunting man ?—the gentlemen departed, whatever the weather : all except a few unsporting " darlings " who had been invited specially to supply a slight admixture of male company to the deserted ladies. The stay-at-homes spent the morning reading, or gossiping, or writing letters at orna-mental tables, until it was time to don tweeds and go out to join the sportsmen, at a spot appointed, in an elaborate, alcoholic lunch. After lunch, a dashing damsel sometimes elected to cower for an hour behind some man as he took aim at the particular bird whose time for slaughter had arrived ; but usually the ladies returned, as they had come, in a body, and spent the time until the men came in for tea changing into luxurious tea-gowns. But a day in the open air did not render the men the liveliest of companions at that exiguous meal ; and it was with relief that everyone went to dress for dinner, with its stimulating, benignant wines. . . .

The annual agricultural show, the flower show at the rectory, a garden party or two constituted the summer entertainment of most young ladies at the beginning of the 'seventies. Church and Sunday-school brought a welcome relief from tedium. Those who had horses at command rode about the country accom-panied by a parent, a brother, or a trusted groom ; or made calls on neighbours within carriage distance. The horseless, however genteel, had no means of locomotion except their own two legs, and these they did not use to excess.

Hunt meets were social occasions which touched with gaiety the lives even of those ladies who did not ride, for a certain rivalry arose between neighbouring houses in the provision of refreshments for the assembled sportsmen and sports-women before they set out on their arduous day. Eventually the occasions blossomed into elaborate champagne breakfasts, which became so big a tax on the pockets of rival hosts that some of the more considerate hunt managers took to calling the meet at a cross-roads or the market place. The annual hunt ball provided those ladies unable to shine in the hunting field with an opportunity to dazzle in the ballroom.

Amateur steeplechasing marked the end of the hunting season. In the 'seventies the races took place across country, and mishaps usually added to the

FAIR TOXOPHILITES: " Archery disciplines the eye, strengthens the muscles and imparts a graceful carriage. Once a year the ladies at the Royal Toxophilite Society have a match to themselves. No gentlemen are permitted except favoured beings styled Captains of the Targets " (1870)

ARCHERY IN REGENT'S PARK: " In the Ladies versus Gentlemen match the latter failed, scoring only 3,294 against the ladies' 3,687, towards which good individual totals of 387 and 386 were contributed by Mrs. Piers Legh and Mrs. Bowley " (1892)

" WATER NYMPHS : A great impetus has been given to ladies' swimming by competitions, which are most varied, as may be seen by our illustrations—(1) some costumes ; (2) the Umpires ; (3) a start ; and (4) diving for eggs and pears " (1883)

excitement—at any rate for the spectators, many of whom were ladies. By the 'nineties a great change had come over these meetings, through the introduction of point-to-point races over artificial courses. As one ardent admirer of the earlier type of meeting lamented in 1894, " the now general adoption of gate money meetings has completely superseded a natural course, and has given us made-up fences and artificial water jumps filled by a water cart on the morning of the race."

Hard frost, which stopped hunting, brought skating. Not that the ladies were adepts as a rule, but they got a good deal of fun and laughter and healthy exercise out of their efforts to emulate the ease with which the men flew over the ice. And on a day of bright sunshine, a picnic lunch at the lakeside, consisting of hot pies and hot coffee, was the accepted way of enlivening a morning's skating. It was not until the 'nineties that women began to take seriously to figure skating. A lady, writing on this fresh aspect, for women, of an old pastime, encouraged the beginner with the statement that " even the best skaters fall when trying any figure that is new to them." She advises her readers to take a fall rather than to try to save themselves, and adds, " although I was once insensible for a short time after falling on the back of my head, and on another occasion, when I fell in the same way, a hairpin made an excursion, or rather incursion, into my head, I have never been so hurt as to be incapacitated from skating again after a short rest."

Our sporting mothers were gallant women.

The 'seventies ushered in the games era which was to bring about such an immense change in the lives of middle and upper class women. It began with croquet, most decorous of games, which could be played—though awkwardly— by ladies in tight bodices, bustles, and flowing skirts. A short golf course for ladies had been laid out at St. Andrews in 1867, and in 1873 feminine golf made its appearance in the south, when a ladies' course was opened at Westward Ho. The golfing girl at first carried but one club, a putter ; but by the 'nineties she possessed a complete battery—and played her way over a full course, North Berwick boasting the best long course for ladies. In 1874 badminton, which rivalled croquet in decorum, was imported from India ; and in 1875 came the momentous introduction of lawn-tennis. Its popularity was instantaneous and widespread, and though prophets foretold its speedy disappearance, it maintained and strengthened its hold on the affections of the young of both sexes, who found a happy meeting ground on the courts that sprang into being in every vicarage garden, every town square.

Stuffy drawing-rooms knew the presence of young ladies no more on fine summer afternoons : they were out on the tennis courts patting the balls softly to and fro. Tennis parties became the rage. The standard of play was not high—the game, after all, was but a pastime. It was left for the twentieth century to elevate it into a sporting science. The net was six inches higher than at

" A LADIES' GOLF MATCH : (1) The method of ' putting.' (2) ' Teeing ' the ball. Golf clubs for ladies are growing, and may in time supersede lawn-tennis clubs. At the Warwickshire Ladies Golf Club competition no fewer than 15 entered " (1889)

present, and in the 'seventies service was always played underhand. An apt beginner could make quite a good showing against a practised opponent ; and it is doubtful whether even the men champions of the 'seventies and 'eighties would have stood much chance against a hard and accurate hitter like Helen Wills, so different was the game in character.

Youths and maidens who had no space in their own gardens for a tennis court or could not afford the price of the nets and posts, formed themselves into sub-scription clubs, and obtained permission to play on public grounds. In the earlier days, ladies were recommended to wear a long pinafore with a big pocket in front to hold the balls not in play. In the 'nineties they were advised to wear " a dark-blue serge skirt, made quite plainly, and fairly short, and of ample width, with a flannel shirt and a sailor hat," and were warned that " care should be taken always to have the cleanest and prettiest of white underskirts, as these show when running for a stroke far more than one would imagine." White shoes were unsuitable as " they make the feet look large." Heelless Russian leather shoes, with red rubber soles, were recommended instead.

Lawn-tennis having opened the eyes of the ladies to the delights of physical activity, their interest began to spread to other games. The influence of the new " public school " type of girls' boarding school weighed in the same side of the scale, for basket ball, rounders, cricket, hockey, lacrosse entered into the games curriculum of such schools as Cheltenham and Wycombe Abbey. Most of the girls who had enjoyed games at school wanted to go on playing them. The educational pundits declared that football was out of the question for girls, but the British Ladies Football Club was founded and played its first match in 1895.

Cricket had a vogue, and no doubt was a great help in promoting the team spirit in the new schools. " Your girls play cricket like gentlemen and behave like ladies," was the admiring comment made to the headmistress by the captain of a ladies' team after her side had suffered defeat against a school eleven. What more could one say in praise of the game ? There were two elevens of profes-sional lady cricketers touring the country in 1890, playing exhibition matches against one another and giving a game to local elevens who offered themselves here and there for slaughter. Clad in " short " white flannel dresses reaching to the ankles and trimmed with red or blue braid according to their side, and wearing white caps adorned with red or blue bows, they made a pretty picture on the cricket pitch.

Cricket clubs for amateur ladies were plentiful. " Every day we find preju-dice yielding to common sense, cricket for ladies becoming more and more popular," writes Lady Milner in 1892. She advised a white flannel skirt of walking length, a well-cut white shirt, a girth belt, and a white sailor hat, tie and hat ribbon in the wearer's club colours, as the ideal cricketing dress. " Let us not spoil our freedom of movement," she continues, " by encasing ourselves in steel armour, more commonly called ' the correct corset.' . . . So much of our success depends on quickness of movement and suppleness of body that I may be pardoned for pointing out that if we are steel-bound and whalebone-lined throughout, the free use of our limbs which the game demands is rendered impossible." Women were undoubtedly advancing towards freedom of the limbs. " Neither should you forget to fasten your hat on securely . . . It is no uncommon thing to see a lady holding on her hat with one hand, striving to catch a ball with the other, and succeeding in doing neither. . . . Boots are better than shoes." She counselled her readers against stopping the ball with their petticoats, " a favourite form of fielding with some lady cricketers," but definitely " bad form " and unworthy of " real cricket." Also, " whatever decision the umpire gives you must implicitly acquiesce in outwardly. We may swear inwardly as much as we like, but if we are given out, out we must go."

The pleasures of swimming began to win appreciation, and though still in the 'nineties most ladies, whether at Brighton or Trouville, confined themselves to bobbing up and down in shallow water at the end of a rope, the more athletic girls were becoming strong swimmers. A sixteen year old follower of the sport swam, for a bet, a quarter of a mile fully clothed. She wore not only " all the ordinary under-garments of a lady, including corsets, but also a heavy, Fishwife serge dress, boots, hat and gloves, carrying in one hand a huge scarlet Turkey twill umbrella opened, and in the other a large bouquet of somewhat gaudy flowers. . . . She of course could not use her arms at all, being obliged to hold them well out of water for the preservation of the umbrella and bouquet, and therefore propelled herself entirely with her legs, arriving on shore safely, amidst the cheers of an admiring crowd." The young lady's sister, Mrs. Samuda, who put this remarkable feat on record, recommends for swimming a bathing dress of Turkey twill made with knickerbockers and a skirt, to be worn with thread stockings, "for decency's sake," and a waterproof cap—an excellent preparation for full dress swimming.

A ladies' eight appeared at Marlow Regatta in 1891, and the following year ladies competed successfully at Wargrave Town Regatta in double-sculling and punting races. " It is clearly to be seen," wrote an enthusiast for the new sport of rowing, that though " twenty years ago it was very different," now " it is the very best thing " for a lady : who should, however, only go on the river suitably attired in plain serge skirt and cotton shirt, " fresh and clean, not tumbled and crumpled, looking as though it had been worn every day and in all weathers from the beginning of the boating season ! "

A girl here and there had—and took—the rare chance of becoming a yachts-woman. Mrs. G. A. Schenley relates how, in the early 'nineties, in one year she " carried off thirty-four prizes—most of them firsts—out of thirty-nine starts, all except two sailed entirely by myself, with no other hand touching the tiller."

Archery, encouraged by the Royal Toxophilite Society of Regent's Park,

" RINGOAL : This game of skill, introduced within the last few years, is a development of the old-fashioned game known as La Grace. In Ringoal, the players endeavour to send the ring with so great a velocity that it cannot be caught by the opposite player but reaches the goal " (1889)

" LADIES' CRICKET : A modification of the game as played by the sterner sex. The wicket is a square board raised some four feet on a pole. Against this the ball is thrown by the bowler" (1889)

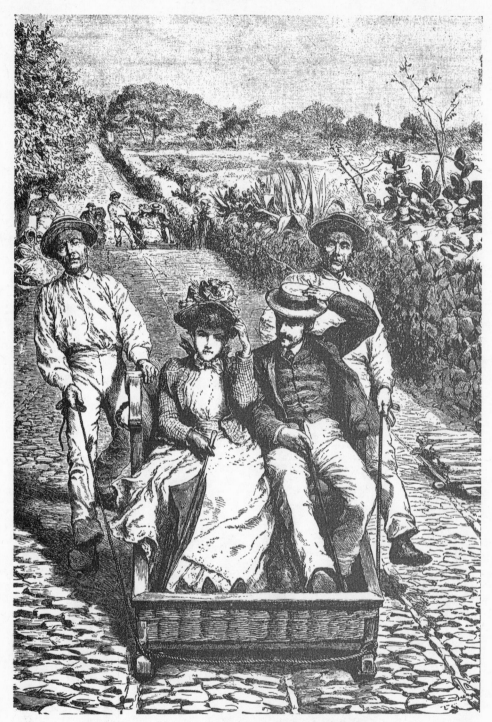

ENGLISH TOURISTS TOBOGGANING IN MADEIRA (1893)

which annually set aside a day in July when ladies from all over England competed for " the handsome prizes so liberally provided by the gentlemen " of the Society, was a serious rival to croquet. It had a number of advantages. One could shoot alone or in company with as many friends as one could persuade to join one. Indifferent marksmanship brought no black looks to the brows of a partner. The practice of the sport involved an amount of exercise too moderate to be fatiguing, and was therefore suitable to ladies of all ages—it was, in fact, never too late to begin. Some of the younger archeresses indulged in summer archery in order to strengthen their arms and wrists for winter hunting. A large enough field and a target or two were the only things necessary to a successful archery party, at which it was usual to shoot off the four dozen arrows at sixty yards before tea, and the two dozen at fifty yards after, " which always seem to be very quickly over and to end only too soon."

Fencing gained some women devotees in the 'nineties—" there is no such nerve tonic, no such bracing occupation as fencing," wrote one feminine lover of the foils, " and one would hear considerably less of hysteria, of morphine-mania, and of other regrettable characteristics of fin-de-siècle existence, if women were to take to fencing as one of the regular occupations of the day."

But fencing was for the few. The sport which set the seal on the average woman's freedom was bicycling. Women had not taken to the old penny-farthing, bone-shaking " ordinary " ; but the coming in the late 'eighties of the safety bicycle, with two equal wheels, opened up a whole new world to them. No longer need the penniless ones sit at home pining for horses to carry them to a longed-for tennis party, a swimming picnic, an archery match. They could jump on the saddles of their metal steeds, and, under their own motive power, spin swiftly along the highways and byways to friendly houses ten—fifteen—twenty miles away. Within a decade, pneumatic tyres, brakes on both wheels, footrests for coasting, and the freewheel were invented, adding still further to the serviceability and popularity of the " bike." Clubs were formed and phalanxes of men and maidens—some of them mounted on the tandem, that famous " bicycle made for two "—bowled away into the country lanes on Sunday mornings. Cycling jaunts were substituted for church going, with undoubted benefit to the health of the young, whatever the effect on their sense of religion. Country clergymen saw to it that there was provision for sheltering the bicycles of cyclists desiring to attend their services. After all, it sometimes rained. . . . Ladies' clubs often took their cycling very seriously. They even went in for racing—a race for ladies was a feature of a cycling meeting at Halensee, near Berlin, in 1895 ; and one of the notable events of a fête held at Carisbrooke Castle in 1899 was a series of bicycle evolutions to music carried out before the Queen by a procession of lady cyclists riding two and two.

"TROUVILLE PLAGE : From the canvas bathing-houses there issue at high water the ladies in 'bloomer' costumes and straw hats, who are careful to let neither their faces nor their hair touch the salt water, who swim with one foot on the bottom, and who never bathe without an escort of male friends. People of all nations saunter along the boarded walk across the sand—Frenchmen in light-blue suits, white boots and small thermometers fastened to their hatbands ; Englishmen in 'loud' patterns ; Russians in top boots, red sashes, and white duck jackets ; Germans in tight trousers ; Swedes, Turks, Americans, Italians, negroes, Cubans " (1874)

"WITH THE QUORN: Brooksby, near Melton, occupied by Mr. Ernest Chaplin, is a favourite meet of the Quorn Hunt. The prominent riders here are Mr. Coupland (the Master), Mr. Chaplin, Lord Wilton, Lady Wilton, Lord and Lady Grey de Wilton, Lord Down, Miss Hartopp, Captain Riddell, Major Tempest, Mr. Behrens, Major Painter, Mr. and Mrs. Lees, Mr. 'Little' Gilmour, Captain Elmhirst and Tom Firr, the golden-mouthed huntsman. The principal hound is old Factor, and behind him is his son Rattler" (1874)

" STEAMING AND PUNTING : Dozens of miniature pleasure steamers, puffing and panting and wheezing, are a new feature of our modern riverside amusements. It is luxurious to steam along in one of these ; but there is still a charm in the old style, and had we the choice we would prefer that broad, slow-going, laborious punt to the swift little iron fish " (1872)

"SATURDAY AFTERNOON AMONG THE HOI POLLOI AT HAMPTON COURT" (1873)

" THE ALL-ENGLAND CROQUET CLUB : This Wimbledon club has a very capital ground laid out in terraces. When our artist visited it for the Spring meeting, each game went quietly on, just as it might in a private garden, except that umpires carried mallets to measure distances, etc. There was a country-rector's-daughter-look about the ladies, while a military element prevailed among a majority of the gentlemen " (1872)

" WINTERING AT HASTINGS : Invalids on the esplanade that fringes the sea margin " (1873)

" SCIENCE AND PLEASURE AT BRIGHTON: Excursions by the British Association " (1872)

" OFF TO THE HIGHLANDS : Odd humans confront lovely nature on the tour from Glasgow to Fort William—strong-minded females with herbariums, alpenstocks, knives, corkscrews, geological hammers and the theoretical intention of roughing it ; victims of the sketching habit, trying to catch the fleeting beauties ; City youths who stalk the deck in impromptu knickerbockers, and imagine themselves Roderick Dhus " (1876)

SIR ROGER DE COVERLEY ON THE ICE NEAR RIPLEY, IN SURREY (1889)

A YACHTING PARTY ON THE NORFOLK BROADS (1890)

" ICE HOCKEY AT WIMBLEDON : Ladies of the Wimbledon Skating Club take advantage of their new privilege of playing hockey. The loose, flowing skirts of these swift Camillas wave gently from side to side in response to the skating motion " (1893)

A LADIES' INTERNATIONAL SKI-ING RACE IN AUSTRIA (1894)

" AT THE FORGE : A first visit to the blacksmith is disquieting when the poor gee-gee submits to a red-hot piece of iron on his foot, which vomits flame and smoke, besides emitting an odour of rancid and terrifying burnt horn " (1890)

" BATHING A LA MODE : The Golden Age Returns, at a Private Pool near Dorking " (1880)

"BOLTED: This is an incident unfortunately by no means uncommon in Rotten Row. In such a frequented spot sights and noises are constantly occurring liable to terrify a nervous horse, and send him tearing off, whither he neither knows nor cares. The poor girl, but for the timely arrival of the gallant officer of police, would be in imminent danger, for she is just in the act of fainting, and, if she were thus to lose her balance, she would be doomed to disfigurement, and possibly death". (1885)

" ' TRACTION-ENGINE, MA'AM ' : An Act of Parliament provides that every locomotive propelled by steam on a public highway must be accompanied by three drivers or conductors ; and that one of these persons must always precede it on foot twenty yards in advance, carrying a red flag, and warning the riders and drivers of horses of the locomotive's approach " (1884)

"A DANGEROUS MOMENT AT A LEVEL CROSSING: Something has frightened the ponies; they will go neither forward nor backward, but remain glued to the metals. The lady seated by the driver looks with terror at the advancing train, and the footman is in the act of descending with the view to forcing the obstinate animals either to advance or retreat" (1889)

A LADIES' DRIVING MATCH AT THE COLOMBO GYMKHANA MEET (1888)

" A LADIES' EGG AND SPOON RACE : A better competition for gymkhana ladies in India
could hardly be imagined than the egg and spoon race on horseback. The distance to be covered
was 300 yards. It was a case where the tortoise beat the hare, for the lady going slowly and sedately
nearly always managed to win" (1895)

" AN INCIDENT WITH THE BELVOIR : A lady's horse threw her off, and in so doing deprived her of the only garment which differentiated her from male followers of the chase. If the skirt had not given she might be now a mangled corpse, instead of escaping with nothing worse than some shapely embarrassment " (1890)

" LAWN-TENNIS IN EGYPT : In place of the Alexandria burnt by Arabi Pasha's ruffians, an imposing city has arisen. Beside the old Ras-el-Teen Fort is a tennis-court, where you can see energetic doubles whenever the heat permits " (1894)

ON WATER : " Happy the grouse ' gun ' who is content with plain water. His surroundings make him safer than most in modern England, where casual water out-of-doors may be noxious through either drainage or factory refuse " (1891)

" MORE LADIES' CRICKET : At country houses the ladies' cricket-match is quite an institution. It is not harder work than lawn-tennis ; it gives opportunity for the wearing of some very pretty costumes ; and it amuses the other sex " (1890)

BLACKBERRYING DELIGHTS IN DEVONSHIRE (1893)

A FRAGRANT LESSON IN BOWLS (1893)

MRS. HULKES'S LEOPARD : " A young leopard having been discovered demolishing a goat carried off overnight, the dogs began to close round him, and the beaters to yell and beat the bush. The leopard broke cover and bounded up a tree. He there presented an easy target, and dropped dead, pierced by a bullet from Mrs. Hulkes, a lady member of the expedition (from India) " (1893)

"A BICYCLING PICNIC NEAR PARIS: The so-called 'rational' costume is affected by the many fashionable ladies who bicycle around Paris, skirts being rarely seen awheel. This is curious, for in London the 'rational' costume never was popular" (1896)

"ROYAL BICYCLISTS: The Hereditary Prince of Saxe-Coburg-Gotha, Princesses Leopoldine of Ratibor, Alexandra and Beatrice of Saxe-Coburg-Gotha, Prince of Hohenlohe-Langenburg" (1896)

" THE PRINCE AS YACHTSMAN : The presence of the Prince of Wales greatly adds to the interest of Riviera regattas, where his *Britannia* carried off every prize for which she competed. His afternoon teas are a very popular daily function " (1894)

V

TOWARDS EMANCIPATION

NONE of the credit for the improvement in women's status during Victoria's reign can be placed to the Queen's personal account. It would be attractive to speculate on what nineteenth century England might have been had her sovereign been an Elizabeth in temperament : a woman in sympathy with all the advancing ideas of her time, and able to use for her own far-seeing ends even those men she personally disliked. Fewer of the Victorians we nowadays call great would have been in conflict with the ideas of the presiding genius of their era ; and the woman's battle would have been won before it began.

Victoria was nearer to another predecessor, Mary II, in her attitude towards her own sex. Strong willed and dominating as she was, she persisted in maintaining the fiction, to herself and others, that she was a " poor weak woman " compelled to overtax her brain by doing work which was properly a man's. The Queen wrote that she was " most anxious to enlist everyone who can speak or write to join in checking this mad, wicked folly of ' Woman's Rights,' with all its attendant horrors. . . . It is a subject which makes the Queen so furious that she cannot contain herself."

But though with the Queen's approval the movement towards emancipation would have swept all opposition away, her disapproval could not stay its rising tide.

There appear to have been two main reasons for the inception of the movement towards women's emancipation at the precise moment which brought it to birth. One was that the effects of the newer education of men were beginning to make themselves felt. Brothers, potential husbands, fathers were, in increasing numbers, brought under the influences emanating from Arnold of Rugby and his contemporaries and followers ; and these reasonably educated young men brought their influence to bear on the reduction of ignorance among their women. For though an ignorant man prefers a wife more ignorant, if possible, than himself, an educated man has little patience, in the long run, with a semi-illiterate woman of slave mentality.

The second great underlying cause of the uprising of women lay not so much in a revolt against the doctrine that woman's place is the home as in an acute realisation by women that, as the century progressed, the country contained ever fewer potential husbands in proportion to the available potential wives. Rather more boys than girls were born then, as now, but more boys than girls succumbed to the dangers of infancy, as they still do ; and in addition there was the tremendous drain of emigration, which affected not only the working class, but the middle and upper classes too. As one old countrywoman remarked to the mother of five growing sons, " these big families, they're bound to be squandered "—and within a few years, one of that family was in New Zealand, a second in the Far East, and a third in the United States. Superfluous younger sons, whose brain power did not suit them for success in industry, turned to Empire building. The black sheep of the family were ruthlessly exported to distant shores. And leaders had to be found for the battalions that waged ceaseless warfare on the Empire's multiple frontiers : between 1849 and 1900, the Indian Government alone engaged in one hundred and ten wars and punitive expeditions. Egypt, the Sudan, the Ashantis, the Zulus—all took their toll of British manhood. " If *we are to maintain* our position as a *first-rate* power, we must, with our Indian Empire and large colonies, be *prepared* for attacks and *wars, somewhere* or *other*, CONTINUALLY," wrote the Queen in 1879. And the many wars of Victoria's reign, fought out invisibly, noiselessly, at a comfortable distance from the homeland, were not therefore bloodless.

> *In vain the laughing girl will lean*
> *To greet her love with love-lit eyes.*
> *Down in some treacherous black ravine,*
> *Clutching his flag, the dead boy lies. . . .*
>
> *For some are by the Delhi walls,*
> *And many in the Afghan land*
> *And many where the Ganges falls*
> *Through seven mouths of shifting sand.*
>
> *And some in Russian waters lie*
> *And others in the seas which are*
> *The portals of the East . . .*

mourned Oscar Wilde in 1881.

Advanced women writers animadverted, not against marriage, but against the fact that so many of their number could not hope for marriage. " A fourth of the women in this country never marry," wrote Frances Power Cobbe. " Men enough to match the women, and a few over to spare, are born into England, but, as each generation ripens into marriageable years, a large proportion of the men and scarcely any of the women have left the country," wrote Augusta Webster. " Colonial frontier men in solitary wilds have few opportunities of courtship or marriage," commented a masculine observer in the 'nineties.

The condition of these unwanted women, unless their fathers were able to leave them a competence, was pitiable. " Women in the educated classes are almost universally taught more or less of some branch or other of the fine arts, but not that they may gain their living or their social consequence," said John Stuart Mill in his *Subjection of Women*. But they were taught nothing else. Ignorant and untrained, they were fit for no employment. They were indeed superfluous.

Hundreds sought to gain a livelihood by governessing. Some of them took to the odious job of acting as companion to an elderly relative or, worse still, a

" HIGHER EDUCATION FOR WOMEN : Girton College is situated some two miles and a half out of Cambridge, and is a brick building in the Gothic style. Its lecture rooms have an air of business, and of grave comfort too " (1877)

" DINING IN HALL, GIRTON : The students dine together, and the discipline imposed upon them is borrowed from colleges devoted to the sterner sex " (1877)

" ADVERSITY : These two sisters have evidently seen better days. The little room is bare, and their black dresses make a sad contrast with the gay ball-dress they are making. The melancholy of their surroundings has come upon the younger sister with full force, and she is appealing for comfort and consolation to the elder one's fortitude " (1891)

" SWEET GIRL GRADUATES AT HOME : Girl students at work in their prettily furnished room inside the recently opened Hall of Residence in Byng Place, Gordon Square, which takes the place of the social amenities of collegiate life—a pressing need since the higher education of young women in London has become more than a possibility " (1883)

stranger. Some turned dressmaker. Some, no doubt, in desperation joined the sisterhood of " fallen women," but history relates nothing of these.

The would-be governesses advertised their desperate need. " A young lady, perfectly competent to teach French, English, and good music wishes to find a situation where there are two or three young children. Salary £25. Protestant and a high character," runs a typical advertisement. From homes where their working time was filled, not too arduously, with womanly occupations, and their leisure with embroidery or macramé work, and money seemed of no importance because it came without effort, girls had to turn into a hard world which often rightly grudged them the miserable wage they asked. Why should it not, when someone else as incompetent could be had for a pound or two less ? " The little civilities—bowings and uncoverings, and openings of doors, and handing of chairs " by which the stronger sex had been accustomed to pay tribute to feminine weakness were gone for ever from their lives. Small wonder that some sought a refuge in ritualist nunneries.

Certain writers, unmindful of Mill, advocated the teaching of a semi-trade such as book-binding or engraving on glass—" a pretty accomplishment and one which, whether practised for pleasure or as a serious trade, can be carried on at home, and by it an income of from a hundred to two hundred a year might be earned by a worker with deft hands, and a little taste and skill in designing." It is surprising that more young women of the day did not hasten to learn so profitable an accomplishment. Widows and deserted wives were in as parlous a state as spinsters who had never been led to the altar. Their hard lot was often complicated by their possession of many children. Mr. E. F. Benson records that his grandmother, left with seven children (the eldest fourteen) and an inadequate provision, was a few years later anxious to start a business for the exploitation of a patent of her husband's. Her eldest son, then in his first year at Cambridge, was horrified at the idea that his mother should embark on " trade " : " It will do me so much harm here, and my sisters so much harm for ever," he remonstrated. His mother dutifully abandoned her sensible scheme. While her eldest son was still at Cambridge, she died, and it was found that she had nothing left except the last payment but one of the annual sum for which she had sold the patent.

Of real education and training, the early Victorian girl had no chance, and most of them gave up all reading except novels as soon as their perfunctory schooling was over. Those, however, who were alive to the crowded state of the marriage market sought to teach themselves if they could get no teaching ; and the most persistent of them, to quote Augusta Webster again, " *stole* it, working surreptitiously over their brothers' discarded schoolbooks and hiding away treatises on metaphysics or astronomy as novelists make naughty heroines hide away French novels."

A few enlightened men, observing the wretchedness of their unmarried sisters, came to the conclusion as early as the late 'forties that an outlet to better things must be provided, and the first material step towards women's emancipation was taken when in 1848 F. D. Maurice founded Queen's College for Women in Harley Street, for the training of governesses. During the first year, two hundred students, women of all kinds and ages, attended. Most of them had already been teaching. Two of the earliest pupils were Frances Mary Buss and Dorothea Beale. Miss Buss began at fourteen to teach in a school run by her mother. At eighteen she took control. She was able to attend only the evening classes at the new College, as she had her own school to run during the day ; but the help she thus received in her own struggles to improve her knowledge heightened her determination that she would alleviate the wretchedness of women of her own class left to fend for themselves. In 1850, at the age of 23, she reorganised her school, and launched it as the afterwards famous North London Collegiate School for Girls.

Miss Beale was born in 1831. She had taught herself Latin and Euclid by helping her brothers with their homework. After a year at Queen's College, she became in 1850 a teacher of mathematics there (which suggests that the standard of teaching was none too high : but where there had previously been nothing at all, one could not hope suddenly for a high standard). She gave up her post in 1856 because she considered that the lady visitors and tutors were allowed too little share in the management of this man-organised college for women. She then spent a wretched year at the school where Charlotte Brontë and her sisters were educated, and in 1858 came her opportunity. She was invited to become the principal of a foundering girls' school opened a year or two previously at Cheltenham. She had an uphill fight to turn it into a success, but she won, and with the opening of the first boarding house in 1864 Cheltenham College for Ladies assumed its place as the first girls' boarding school of " public school " type.

The lack of trained teachers was one of the greatest difficulties with which these educational pioneers had to contend ; but the years went on, and this difficulty diminished as teachers from Queen's College and Bedford College for Ladies (founded the year after Queen's by a woman, Mrs. Reid, and run by a mixed board of management) became available. With the creation of the Girl's Public Day School Trust in 1872, secondary education for girls ceased to be an idea of ridiculous absurdity, and became an established fact ; and though many years were to pass before it became as usual for the girls of a family as the boys to receive a secondary education, the possibility was there.

The next fortress confronting the women who desired to learn was that of higher education. This proved harder to capture than the first. It could be successfully demonstrated that in giving girls some kind of secondary education, there was no idea of setting them up against boys. They were taught different subjects by different methods : Miss Beale found that under the heading of physical geography, a subject seldom taught to boys, she was able to teach her girls a good many subjects which under less general headings would have met

"THE PEERESSES' GALLERY : These fair ladies, drawn at the opening of Parliament, look down on the Lords under rights acquired before the Norman Conquest. The Peers wisely respect this privilege, though the unwise Commons for about a century have exiled the ladies from their gallery. What is the result of that discourtesy ? The crusade of ' Woman's Rights,' the effort which women will shortly make to obtain seats in Parliament itself. Had the present occupant of the Chair in the Commons been able to remark, as did one of his predecessors, ' I am sure I see petticoats,' the Lower House would be spared its fear of such invasion " (1872)

WAR CORRESPONDENCE: " Lady Florence Dixie, correspondent of *The Morning Post* during the campaign against Boers, visited Cetewayo in confinement near Cape Town. She reported that some Zulu chief men wished to have their King back, and Cetewayo exclaimed, ' I am sure it is the wish of the Zulu nation that I should return ; it is only those frightened by John Dunn that oppose the restoration of my rulership ' " (1882)

with parental disapproval. To demand admission to university examinations was a different matter.

The pioneer in the movement for higher education was Emily Davies. She had been drawn into the movement through the friendship of her brother Llewelyn with F. D. Maurice. Her campaign was opened publicly at the Social Science Congress of 1862, when Miss Cobbe read a paper on women in relation to the universities, and was greeted with "universal ridicule." Not quite universal, however, for a committee to secure the admission of women to university examinations was formed, with Emily Davies as its secretary. To her grateful surprise, she found the idea met with a friendly reception among the younger professors at several universities. Cambridge Syndicate was approached, and in 1863, six weeks before the date of the Local Examinations, agreed to hand the papers to the committee, which had to organise the examination of the girls and make its own arrangements with the examiners for the correcting of papers. In spite of the short time at their disposal, the committee rounded up ninety-one candidates, who did fairly well in some subjects, but failed lamentably in arithmetic. The first impact with an outside standard showed at once the low level of the best girls' educational attainments. Three years later, the Cambridge Local Examinations were thrown open officially to girls, and the women had won the preliminary round in the battle for higher education.

The next move made by Miss Davies was to advocate a residential college for ladies run on university lines and with university standards. She got together another committee, the men on which proved almost too ardent in their support and the women too lukewarm. She was, indeed, decidedly critical of the youth of the university dons who wanted to come on her committee and help her to realise her project. She was always a stickler for propriety, and when in 1869 she took a lease of Benslow House at Hitchin and organised an entrance examination for students, she remarked of the six candidates admitted, "Those we are sure of are all past twenty and look like discreet young women." In 1870, after five of her students had passed a Little Go privately organised for them, the difficulties of running her college so far from the University proved so great that she bought land at Girton, two miles from Cambridge—far enough to give "the necessary feeling of safety to parents," near enough to enable lectures to go forward without hindrance. The girls moved into their new building in 1873. Thus began Girton.

Meanwhile in the North of England a series of lectures for women on astronomy had been organised under the enthusiastic leadership of Anne Jemima Clough and Mrs. Josephine Butler, whose husband at that time was Principal of Liverpool College. Miss Clough, born in 1820, was the sister of one of Dr. Arnold's favourite pupils. The lectures were filled to overflowing, and three hundred sets of written answers to a set of written questions were showered upon Mr. (afterwards Professor) James Stuart, the astonished lecturer. The North of England Council, as the organising committee was called, requested

Cambridge to set a special examination to test the progress of its students, a request granted in 1869. The examination thus begun specially for women was, five years later, thrown open to men also, and became known as the Higher Local Examination. The lectures eventually merged into the University Extension scheme for both men and women ; but not before they had been introduced into Cambridge itself by Mr. (afterwards Professor) Sidgwick, who had married one of the Garrett sisters. Eighty ladies attended the first course, and in the following year (1871) a house was taken to board five students, and put under the control of Miss Clough. Thus began Newnham.

The development of the women's colleges at Oxford followed similar lines. Lectures had been started there at about the same time as in Cambridge, but had petered out. In 1872 a second series began and persisted, until in 1879 Lady Margaret Hall and Somerville were opened to accommodate resident students.

A Grace brought forward in the Cambridge Senate in 1873, proposing that the Tripos Examinations should be opened to women, was rejected ; but the same arrangement for private examination was allowed as in the case of Little Go. Miss Davies sent in three candidates : two secured seconds and one a third. The Tripos Examinations were thrown open to women in 1881 ; and three years later Oxford, with Mr. Gladstone's blessing, admitted women to most of the examinations for honours. But proposals to admit women to degrees were rejected, again and again, by both Oxford and Cambridge.

The throwing open of degrees to women at other universities is connected with the struggle for medical training, which proved the hardest round in the educational fight. Dr. Elizabeth Blackwell, who had secured her degree in America, placed her name on the British Medical Register in 1859. She was one of the last doctors to do so in virtue of a foreign degree, for during the following year the medical profession secured a new charter excluding holders of only foreign degrees. The young Elizabeth Garrett came into contact with Dr. Blackwell, and was fired by ambition to follow in her footsteps. Helped and encouraged by her father, she set about her aim. She found that the only way on to the British Medical Register lay through the Apothecaries' Examination, which she passed ; subsequently she took a Paris M.D. Four more young women successfully presented themselves for the Apothecaries' Examination. In face of this impending invasion, the authorities took steps to make it legally impossible for further women to get on to the British Medical Register in this indirect way.

But the woman who won medical training for women was yet to enter the ring. She was Sophia Jex-Blake, a fiery and not always discreet advocate of women's advancement. She became a lecturer in mathematics at Queen's College at the age of nineteen, and her career seemed set for education. Then, during a journey in America, she met a follower of Dr. Blackwell's, and her thoughts turned to medicine. On her return to England, she canvassed all the available possibilities of training, and decided that Edinburgh seemed to offer the best chance. She went there in 1869 and managed to organise studies for

"A PARLIAMENTARY CAGE: The Ladies' Gallery in the Commons has three rows, but there might as well be only one. From the front, as much can be seen and heard as from any other position in the House. From the second row only the floor space between gangway and door is visible. The back row represents the 'vanishing point' of sight and sound " (1889)

" WOMEN'S SUFFRAGE : The St. James's Hall meeting to support franchise for women house-holders was presided over by Mrs. Garrett Anderson, M.D. Other enthusiasts above are the Misses Lydia Becker, Edith Simcox, and Eliza Orme, Mrs. Oliver Scatchard, Mrs. Ashton Dilke, Lady Goldsmid, and Mr. J. P. Thomasson, M.P. The speeches were sedate in tone " (1884)

" ARCTIC CONSTITUTIONAL : Lieutenant Peary was accompanied by his young, recently married wife in his discovery of the northern boundary of Greenland. She is the first lady in any Polar expedition. Every day the Pearys took long walks on snowshoes " (1892)

herself and several other women students in a similar private way to that adopted by Miss Davies at Cambridge. Some of the professors were not unfavourable to women ; but the legal difficulties which Miss Jex-Blake and her fellows had to overcome proved insuperable. She came back to London, and with pioneer audacity decided that if women could not gain admittance to the recognised places of medical instruction, she would organise a place for women alone. She took a house in Hunter Street, and, with the help of Elizabeth Garrett (by then Mrs. Garrett Anderson) developed her scheme into the London School of Medicine for Women.

She and her friends had secured, in the meantime, the introduction into Parliament of the Enabling Bill, which empowered universities, if they so desired, to grant degrees to women. It passed in 1875 ; and the King's and Queen's College of Physicians in Dublin immediately consented to examine women and grant them medical degrees. The Royal Free Hospital agreed to accept students from the women's new medical school ; and London University, which had thrown open its doors to women students in 1869, granted medical and other degrees to women in 1880. The provincial universities followed suit.

Having become educated, the young ladies of the later years of the century sought outlets for their energies. Most women graduates became teachers, and for many years the schools were able to absorb all the competent women available. Their monetary rewards were not large. Under the London School Board, which paid the highest salaries, a trained assistant mistress began, in 1894, at £85 a year ; and headmistresses received from £200–£300 a year. The average well-educated, successful assistant mistress seldom earned more than £150 a year, after years of experience. An increasing number of women entered journalism. Fashion was already recognised as peculiarly their province ; and the *Daily News* was represented in Paris during the 'nineties by a woman.

A few women took appointments as managers of settlements in the London slums, and the woman preacher was not unknown. Millinery and dressmaking establishments were opened by women of birth. The admission of women to clerkships in the Post Office Savings Bank in 1881 marked their entry into the Civil Service ; while the modern typewriter, introduced in 1878, was the key to still another department of labour for middle-class women. Once the barriers went down, women began to find opportunities of employment in often unexpected quarters, " simply because employers are beginning to think it to their interest to employ cheaper and more tractable workers than they usually find in men." . . .

Next to education, and their consequent ability to obtain money-making employment, the most important gain of women in the Victorian era was the command secured by married women over their own earnings and possessions. The Marriage and Divorce Act of 1857 (against one clause of which Mr.

Gladstone made twenty-nine speeches) established a separated wife's right to possess her future earnings or inheritance.

The Married Women's Property Act of 1870 conferred certain property rights on a wife : her wages and earnings became her own ; so did deposits made in savings banks, and personal property or rents and profits devolving on her, if married after the Act, as next of kin of an intestate, or any sum up to £200 coming to her under a will or deed. The Act of 1882 conferred on a married woman the same rights of acquisition and ownership as if she were a " feme sole " (a single woman) ; while the Act of 1893 made it clear that contracts entered into by a married woman, except as an agent, were in respect of her own property alone.

Politically the period was one of feminine disappointment. The idea of woman's suffrage was by no means generally antipathetic—the *Queen* newspaper, which appealed especially to leisured and moneyed women, was already in the 'sixties a strong advocate of votes for women. Eight women actually voted in Manchester in 1868, and several in London. Of three whose voting was observed, two attended together, and one alone. They gave their numbers, stated for whom they wished to vote (it was four years before the introduction of the secret ballot), and left quietly without exciting any remark, although one of the reasons constantly urged against allowing women to vote was that they would be subject to all kinds of indignities at the polling booths. This sort of thing was said even after women had secured the municipal franchise (1869) and had been given the power to vote for and sit on the school boards set up in 1870.

The first society for female suffrage was formed at Sheffield in 1857, but the matter became a live issue only with John Stuart Mill's election to Parliament in 1865. He had included woman's suffrage in his election address. The National Society for Women's Suffrage was founded in 1867 (Florence Nightingale was its most notable member), and in the same year Mill presented the first petition to Parliament. Petitions with an average of 200,000 signatures a year were for many years continually being forwarded to Parliament. In 1870 the second reading of the Women's Disabilities Bill was carried by 33 votes. Mr. Gladstone, who feared to invite woman " unwittingly to trespass upon the delicacy, the purity, the refinement, the elevation of her own nature," strongly opposed the bill, which was lost in committee by 220 votes to 94. Next year the same bill was lost by 220 to 151. Trevelyan's Household Franchise Bill of 1873 raised false hopes in the women, strengthened by Mr. Joseph Chamberlain's carrying a resolution in favour of woman's suffrage at a great Liberal meeting at Birmingham. The franchise was conferred on women in the Isle of Man in 1880. Bills and resolutions were brought forward year after year by devoted masculine adherents of woman's suffrage, but they never got beyond a second reading. The last bill of the century, introduced in 1897, passed its second reading with a majority of 71, and then disappeared. It was left to the twentieth century to secure political equality.

" A LADY PLAGUE-DOCTOR : A plague camp has been constructed at Khana, about 100 miles from Calcutta. Every train is stopped, and passengers are given close medical scrutiny. A lady doctor examines the lady passengers, no matter when the train arrives " (1897)

" HORSE DOWN : The horse is not hopelessly down, and if those two or three volunteers will hang on behind, it will be pulled up willy-nilly. The old lady, meanwhile, has excited the jeers of messenger boys by her singularity in travelling alone in a hansom " (1872)

" TILE-PAINTING FOR FEMALES : The coloured wall-tiles in the new refreshment rooms of the South Kensington School of Art are being painted by female students, under an Art Master. During our visit some of the young artists were filling in spaces with pleasant fountains with rims that held stately peacocks. Others were producing panels of fruits and flowers in great profusion. We congratulate the Schools of Art on their success in thus affording a new and interesting occupation for talented young women " (1870)

MRS. JOPLING DEMONSTRATES : " Mrs. Jopling has combined with her extensive practice
in portrait painting a system of instruction in one lesson. Standing before her pupils, she seeks to
demonstrate all her artistic secrets, so that the pupils can practise to do likewise " (1887)

"A PERIPATETIC LECTURER : The five peripatetic lecturers taking classes round the British Museum Galleries, giving discourses and explaining the marbles, include one lady, who takes female visitors only. There is also a Cambridge man, who takes both sexes indiscriminately" (1881)

"A ROYAL ARTIST : The Princess Louise, when in Quebec, takes her 'studio in waiting' in tow of her steam launch. A steam-tug, not knowing H.R.H., gave her its back-wash. Her A.D.C. sculled out of the billows, but back came the Princess, as cool as you please, in the cause of art" (1883)

" A FRENCHWOMAN'S PERIL: Monsieur and Madame Duruof drifted the whole night, and then descended into the North Sea. They were dragged for two hours, half under water, before the captain and mate of the *Grand Charge* saved them at great peril. Whatever one may think of this rash risk in a balloon, there is but one opinion respecting the gallant English sailors " (1874)

" CATHERINE BOOTH ON TRIAL: The Swiss authorities, losing patience with Miss Booth for her defiance of decrees against the Salvation Army, arrested her with 'Captain' Becquet and others. A Geneva jury found the prisoners 'not guilty,' and they were released " (1883)

" CALISTHENICS : The centenary of the Royal Masonic School for Girls was celebrated by a great Masonic Festival in the Albert Hall. The Prince of Wales gave his opinion that the girls performed their calisthenic exercises and drill very methodically " (1888)

" FEMALE CHORISTERS : St. Paul's Pro-Cathedral, Melbourne, has boldly thrown all ecclesiastical traditions aside, and introduced lady choristers in surplice and rounded trencher. The effect was admirable on the whole, though Church composure was ruffled in some instances " (1887)

"VISCOUNTESS FOLKESTONE'S ORCHESTRA: The Viscountess Folkestone's band numbers many ladies of the nobility, and comprises fourteen first and thirteen second violins, eight violas, eight violoncellos, and even three lady players of that cumbrous instrument, the double bass. It was a very pretty sight to see her executants, whose delicious first concert was attended by the Prince and Princess of Wales." (1884)

" LONDON'S SCHOOL BOARD : The lady members are prominent, including Mrs. Surr, who is speaking, Miss Helen Taylor, and Mrs. Fenwick-Miller. Mrs. Westlake is an earnest champion of what Mrs. Fenwick-Miller has dubbed ' the official ring.' Miss Muller and Miss Simcox are both good workers on the Board, and Miss R. Davenport Hill, Mrs. Webster, and Miss Richardson are quiet helpers " (1882)

"ON THE BOULEVARDS: Of all the sights afforded by Paris none makes such an impression on tourists, by daylight or gaslight, as the inner line of Boulevards. Persons of both sexes are in the magnificent cafés. The liquids they consume range from the rich brown of chocolate to the scarlet of syrup, the gold of Chartreuse, and the deadly green of absinthe " (1877)

"THE ALHAMBRA'S MODERN GOTHS : Friends of these tourists will smile with ridicule on seeing 'Pa' and 'Maud' photographed on a background of the Court of Lions ; but it is only those that chip off mementos who deserve the title of 'Goths'" (1890)

"A NEW TELEPHONE EXCHANGE : It is an extraordinary feat that two persons at a distance are enabled to converse. In an ' exchange,' the ' switch-board ' attendant switches the subscriber to a table-operator, who calls his required number to the first attendant, who connects the subscribers' pair of lines by means of corresponding plugs " (1883)

"FAIR ICONOCLASTS : Monuments and temples up the Nile are rapidly being mutilated by relic-hunters, largely females, we regret to say. Ladies belonging to the personally-conducted parties are constantly engaged in depredations similar to that in our illustration " (1890)

" AN UNWELCOME INTERRUPTION : Bacchus as an election agent is discredited. ' Treating '
is prohibited, but coaxing is still legitimate. When a lady, whose charm has not been sterilised by
close study of her subject, adjures an elector to vote for Mr. ——, just to please herself, the con-
victions of a lifetime are apt to totter. But all party-managers do not select their canvassers so
wisely and tactfully, as our sketch above shows " (1892)

MR. GLADSTONE'S VISITATION: "Deputations from the ladies of Ireland were received by
Mr. and Mrs. Gladstone at Hawarden. Mrs. Kate Sullivan, Lady Mayoress of Dublin, read a brief
address for Home Rule, signed by 400,000 Irishwomen. Mr. Gladstone replied in a neat little speech
which lasted over an hour and a quarter" (1886)

MRS. PANKHURST AT HOME: " A Conference of the Women's Franchise League, lasting three evenings, was held at the Russell Square house of Dr. and Mrs. Pankhurst. It demanded no less for women than ' equal civil and political rights with men ' " (1891)

FEMALE ACADEMICALS: " Of the new Bachelors of Arts from London University 53 were ladies. Five ladies also took the M.A. degree, and 3 headed the list " (1891)

"NURSES AT MARLBOROUGH HOUSE: The Prince addressed the nurses in a very informing speech on their certificates of good collection for their own Pension Fund" (1890)

" A LADIES' FIRE-BRIGADE : Twenty-six young ladies have volunteered to man a ' Lillie '
fire-engine for the Marazion Brigade. Unmistakable evidence of their efficiency was given at St.
Michael's Mount, when these staunch fire-fighters worked their engine and went through a series
of performances in sheet-holding, sheet-jumping and ladder-scaling " (1893)

ART STUDENTS EXULT OVER MAFEKING : " The South Kensington Art Schools have finely helped to celebrate the relief of Mafeking. Men and girls in modelling blouses followed a young rider made up as Lord Roberts. A colossal bust of Colonel Baden-Powell—the work of several students—was set high on a chair " (1900)

MAFEKING BACCHANTES : " Friday night's enthusiasm over the joyful news from Mafeking did not abate on Saturday, when cheering, flag-waving, singing crowds paraded in the open spaces of Trafalgar Square, which were choked by surging masses. Women in particular relieved their exulted feelings by inviting strangers to dance wildly in the centre of the square " (1900)

VI

GOOD WORKS AND SWEET CHARITY

Every Victorian lady read her New Testament, and was convinced that she lived her life in accordance with its teachings. She was sublimely unconscious that the system of morals by whose guidance she trod was erected on a basis of selected passages from the Good Book; and that among those selected passages some at least were not, perhaps, accurately interpreted. She read in her Bible, not once, but thrice, " The poor ye have always with you," and she took this to mean, " The poor ye shall always have with you." She also read, " Sell all that thou hast, and give to the poor," but that passage so obviously referred to a particular young man far away in ancient Palestine that it could have no bearing on Victorian England. A few cranks like Charles Kingsley and F. D. Maurice had the presumption to believe that if the one passage were to be read in as the continuous present, the other should be likewise understood.

Happily for the mental comfort of the middle and upper classes, such literal minded parsons were in the minutest minority, and one could perform one's religious duties satisfactorily without paying any attention to their disturbing theories. Certainly it was the duty of a Christian to do something about the poor, which term was understood by the majority of Ladies Bountiful, in full agreement with Queen Victoria herself, as the *clean* poor. The squire's wife, the parson's wife (when not an object of charity herself), and the schoolmaster's wife, together with their respective daughters, all exercised their charitable impulses on their village neighbours. Cotton blankets and red flannel petticoats at Christmas, a pound of cheap tea now and again, a bowl of soup in time of sickness, and an ounce or two of tobacco for the good man's pipe : these simple remedies for relieving the miseries of family life on 12s. a week gave complete rest to the conscience of the Victorian lady during the months she spent in the country. Some, more self-sacrificing than the rest, visited the poor in their homes, and sat, for as long as an hour, in the fetid atmosphere of rooms whose windows would not open, by the side of bedridden old men or women, reading aloud from some tract or other godly work. The self-allotted penance over, the charitable visitor escaped with relief, and forgot, until her next visitation was due, the existence of the unfortunate creatures destined to lie in unwholesome air until death released them.

The children were encouraged in charity by admonitions to put on one side for the gardener's little daughter, or the crippled son of the blacksmith, those toys of which they had tired, or which had been broken beyond repair. The clothes and boots they had outgrown, and such of mamma's dresses and shawls as could scarcely be turned to further use by herself or her family, were likewise passed on to the poor. Thus, at small expense, the cause of sweet charity was served.

Those who had wealth and some enlightenment sometimes went in for more

" CHRISTMAS VISITING : The young ladies from the Manor House, visiting their humble
neighbours, take with them a bottle of port as balm for the old man's rheumatic pains, tea and sugar
for his wife, small groceries and toys for the children. Above all, the smiles of the joyous girls
will cheer their old neighbour for the Battle of Labour and Sorrow to which he must return " (1870)

THE VICAR'S CLUSTER : FLORAL DECORATIONS FOR CHRISTMAS (1870)

extensive schemes which were of benefit not only to the poor, but also to their benefactors. The Dowager Countess of Jersey speaks of a school established by her mother-in-law for training the village girls as servants, over which, in the early days of her marriage, she herself was called to preside " at an age which I should have considered hardly sufficient for a second housemaid." But to be born within the circle of the Upper Ten Thousand, or near it, was to be endowed by Providence with a superiority of soul which enabled one, oneself untaught, to teach others.

Nor was there neglect of suitable openings for charitable work in Town. The Franco-German War of 1870 was an opportunity for ladies to gather themselves together to manufacture comforts and bandages for the sick and wounded on both sides—" medical stores which I fancy would have been to a large extent condemned wholesale if submitted to the medical authorities during the late war, but which I am sure were very useful and acceptable in '70–71," wrote one who helped in this impartial well-doing.

Then there were the hospitals. According to a gentleman who in 1897 surveyed, with much complacence, the social transformations of the Victorian Age : " Like all gracious works, these places are twice blessed. They relieve those who are in need. They humanise those whom prosperity and comfort might make callous. Before our age began, no one thought of sending game or fruit to the sufferers or convalescents within these places of refuge. Now it is the exception for the millionaire not to make the spoils of his fashionable battue pay tithe to those for whom such food is often the best of physic. The costly flowers that decorate the drawing-rooms or dining-rooms during the season are not discarded as rubbish when the festivity is over. They are scrupulously tended so as not to lose their freshness. Presently their hues and fragrance will relieve the bleak expanse of white-washed wall in those places where our sick are nursed away from their own homes." And if the millionaire himself did not attend to these little details, his wife certainly did.

She went even further, for by the beginning of the 'nineties she and her friends began to organise and take part in street collections for the hospitals.

In the 'eighties, doing good became positively fashionable. The Princess of Wales headed a branch committee of the National Aid Society which included Lady Salisbury, Lady Rosebery, Mrs. Gladstone, and Miss Nightingale among its members. It proposed to provide comforts and nursing for those who fell sick and wounded in Egypt while serving with the Gordon Relief Expedition. It is a little strange to find the name of Florence Nightingale, who had removed good works from the trivial plane of the Ladies Bountiful into high politics, among these earnest committee-women ; but the fact that one of their aims was to provide trained nursing for her beloved soldiers overcame her reluctance. In the same year, the Prince of Wales presided over the Dilke Commission of inquiry into the housing of the poor.

The Duchess of Teck collected among her friends for Miss Ada Leigh's work among women in Paris, and " with her usual consideration restricts the subscription to £5 or alternatively as making less demand on donors' means £1 every twelve-months for a five years' period." Lord Randolph Churchill found time while launching the new party of his day to serve on a committee organised by his mother the Duchess of Marlborough for the relief of distress in Ireland, and lent his aid to the popularising of those slumming expeditions which enjoyed such a vogue in the 'eighties and 'nineties. While Mr. Joseph Chamberlain was building orchid houses out of the profits made from the nail-making trade in which women earned 3s. to 5s. a week, his sister did not hesitate to co-operate with other ladies of Birmingham in systematic house to house visitation of the poor in order to " instruct the wives and daughters of working men in the arts of domestic management, and in the possibility of keeping the humblest homes happy, healthy, comfortable and clean." Long before infant welfare had been imagined, Mrs. Humphry Ward wrote a leaflet called " Plain Facts on Infant Feeding," and circulated it in the slums of Oxford—a refreshing instance of commonsense aid among the often unpractical well-doing of the period.

The Queen went down to a well washed and brushed up East End to open the People's Palace in 1887 ; and, in harmony with the wave of benevolence which swept over landed proprietors in the latter half of the reign, she threw open to the public Windsor Park and the gardens and terraces of the Castle, so that excursionists could view the beauties of the royal estate or listen to the band on the terrace playing Her Majesty's favourite airs.

Ladies in Belgravia invited the guttersnipes of the neighbourhood to tea in the drawing-room, and, when the guests proved too wilfully disinclined to respond to the good that was being done them, had them removed along with the tea things. Ladies also organised drawing-room meetings to raise funds for missions to the heathen abroad and to fallen women at home. They founded clubs for the working girls of Soho and Mayfair where on Sundays they taught them the Bible, and on weekdays, after work was over at 7 or 8 o'clock, gave them lessons in needlework, history, reading, writing, arithmetic and singing. Three branches of the Needlework Guild, founded by Lady Wolverton to provide comfortable clothing for orphans, accumulated during 1892 more than seventy thousand garments. To a would-be organiser of a Dorcas Society, the editor of a popular woman's weekly wrote, " I take it that ' Tabitha ' would have the clothes made by ladies ; it is an advantage to the poor to have their things properly cut out and made."

The craze for slumming led to the formation of an immense variety of societies, all of which aimed at the moral betterment of the poor—some overtly, and some under the guise of helping them to physical betterment. The main aim of a large proportion of them was, under cover of benevolence, to supply cheap and docile domestic labour. The Baroness Burdett-Coutts, who in 1871 had been created a peeress in her own right in recognition of her vast charitable works, took the lead in the organisation of many of these societies. She was, for instance, the president of the Destitute Children's Dinner Society which in 1891 provided 290,476 dinners in fifty-five dining-rooms in various parts of

IMPARTIAL AID: " The Ladies' Committee of the National Aid Society has prepared abundant linen, lint and bandages, for distribution with the utmost impartiality to the French and German armies, after the battles of Sedan and Montmédy " (1870)

A PRINCESS'S CHARITY : " Princess Christian, a district visitor at Windsor, is the first daughter of any English monarch to undertake such a task. Basket in hand, she administers kind counsel and creature comforts to the poor of twenty cottages " (1888

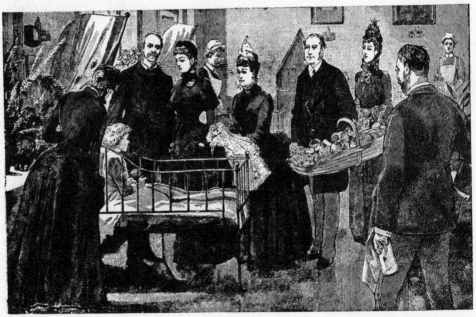

A DIVA'S CHARITY : " Madame Albani gratified a desire to help the Jenny Lind Infirmary by visiting Norwich, with Mr. Santley, Mr. Edward Lloyd, and Lady Benedict. The result was a splendid and profitable concert in that ancient city. The diva took a huge basket of toys, which she distributed with kindly words " (1886)

London at a charge of a halfpenny each. The meal consisted of a plateful of stew—beef or mutton, potatoes, barley or rice, and onions—and a substantial slice of bread. " Clean faces and hands, orderly manners at table, are insisted upon ; grace is sung by the children before and after the meal, thus utilising the charity as a moral influence for good as well as a material benefit," wrote Mrs. Molesworth in describing this society. Did the children always intone the words they were instructed to use, or had they some more ribald version of their own ? . . . Yet they were the children of their age, and probably the half-starved young things responded in the way anticipated.

The provinces were not behind the metropolis in their efforts to do good to the children. The German miner quoted in a previous chapter notes : " Several benevolent societies in Newcastle resolved in October 1896 to give shoes and stockings to three thousand poor children who were to be selected by the school teachers. I must say, nothing better could have been fixed upon, for it is very difficult in large working-class families to replace the shoes worn out in playing with preserved meat tins in the streets." The same observer records the establishment by Lord Armstrong of a technical and an elementary school, both free to every one, and not only to the benefactor's workmen, and of a childrens' hospital erected by Lady Armstrong—" one of the handsomest buildings in the city, and it is free to those without means."

The Children's Happy Evenings Association organised indoor games, accompanied by moral instruction, in order to get slum children out of the streets at night. The Metropolitan Association for Befriending Young Servants constituted itself the general protector of all young servants in London between the ages of 13 and 20. The Girls' Friendly Society, founded in 1857, provided social amenities and good advice for servant girls. These last two organisations insisted upon an unblemished reputation as a condition of membership ; but the Ladies' Association for the Care of Friendless Girls held out a hand to those " on whom the world is inclined to look askance," and helped slightly fallen girls to recover their self-respect—in domestic service. The Mothers Union united all mothers in prayer for the better upbringing of their children. Mothers of the higher class received a different card from the others, with a prayer adapted to their special needs. The Guernsey Society for Supplying Needlework to the Respectable Poor was founded in 1886 with the object of supplying women of good character with needlework in their homes during the winter months.

Sailors' Homes, " on broad lines, undenominational, catholic, bright, teetotal, with (if possible) a personal and motherly element pervading them " were brought into being in the home ports. Like true Britons, their patronesses carried their native customs overseas and in the ports of the Orient established mission rooms where a wandering sailor who had not seen a woman for fifteen months would suddenly find himself on his knees beside a stylishly dressed lady who prayed for his especial welfare—that he might, in the words of a contemporary writer, " be indeed the brave, true, God-fearing man that can guard his country or extend her commerce." Some at least of these godless wanderers took the spiritual consolations offered in good part, left most of their earnings in the safe keeping of their lady well-wishers, and went to the houses down the road for the human comfort their bodies craved.

More serious in quality were the settlements and missions established in the East End where students from Cheltenham and from the women's colleges of Oxford and Cambridge vied with Oxford and Cambridge men in solemn self-dedication to the impossible task of adapting comfortable middle class christianity to the aching poverty of the slums. Which was the greater marvel—the pitiful patience of the poor in not rising to rend these well meaning interlopers from another plane ; or the incredible courage of the missionary zealots who dared to enter the filthy alleys and noisome dens in which men and women, brutalised by excess of poverty, hid their vile bodies and viler habits ? The sole explanation of the strange phenomenon of Victorian charity, in all its phases, lies in the complete, unquestioning certainty of rich and poor alike that the two sections of society were fashioned of different clay.

Strong in this conviction, East End settlement workers from the universities felt that they were giving, in the words of a contemporary, " the poorest and most densely populated working class districts the benefit of a resident gentry " ; and ladies could unhesitatingly write such expressions as " I had caught the ' navvy fever,' " used by Mrs. Charles Garnett in describing the work of the Christian Excavators' Union. Even to the most sincere and simple of well-doers, their beneficiaries had their due place in the world, and must keep it : they were underdogs, and underdogs they must remain. Their worst ills might be relieved ; they might be encouraged to godliness, to thrift, to sobriety ; they might be treated occasionally to a day in the country or a Christmas feast ; but they ought never to think of comparing their lives of privation with the lives of ease enjoyed by their betters. The poor, on the whole, acquiesced, dumbly, uncomprehendingly, in these assumptions. It was not among them that republican sentiments were rife, but among the artisans and skilled workers just above the poverty line. The idea of human equality was as far from the minds of the very poor as from those of their benefactors.

CHARITY AND JEWISH INFANTS: "The annual ball in aid of the Jews' Infant Schools was successful in all respects and the collection amounted to about £500. We cannot help remarking on the spirit of charity which characterises the Hebrew community. If Christian charities were proportionately as extensive and well organised, the misery which disgraces our great city would be considerably lessened" (1872)

THE QUEEN'S LITERARY GIFT : " The Queen, with Princess Beatrice and Prince Leopold, and attended by Lady Waterpark, Major-General Ponsonby and Colonel the Hon. H. Byng, visited military invalids from the Ashanti War at Netley Hospital. Next day the patients received from Osborne copies of ' Leaves from my Journal in the Highlands,' with an inscription in the Queen's own handwriting " (1874)

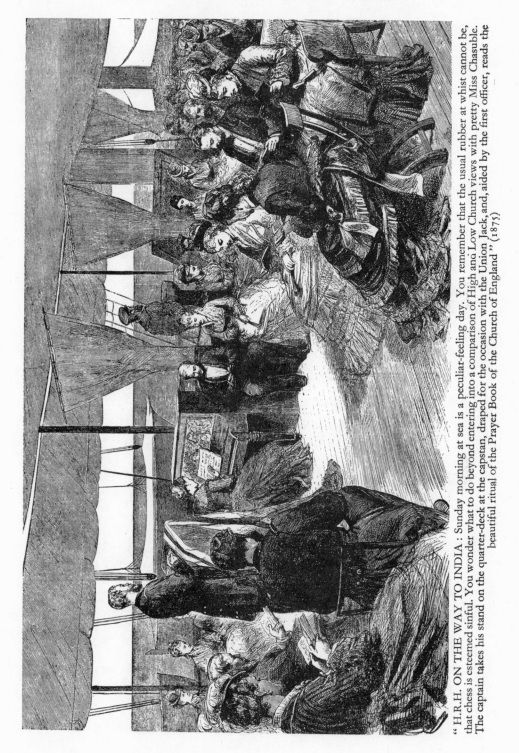

" H.R.H. ON THE WAY TO INDIA : Sunday morning at sea is a peculiar-feeling day. You remember that the usual rubber at whist cannot be, that chess is esteemed sinful. You wonder what to do beyond entering into a comparison of High and Low Church views with pretty Miss Chasuble. The captain takes his stand on the quarter-deck at the capstan, draped for the occasion with the Union Jack, and, aided by the first officer, reads the beautiful ritual of the Prayer Book of the Church of England " (1875)

"THE IRISH RELIEF COMMITTEE: Charitable ladies and gentlemen working with the Duchess of Marlborough in Dublin for the relief of Ireland's distressed poor. From the left, going round the table—Miss Trench, Mr. Fitzgerald, Miss Fitzgerald, Hon. Mrs. O'Hagan, Miss Hillier, Hon. Mrs. Robinson, Dr. Meredith, Lady Michel, the Duchess of Marlborough, Dr. Grimshaw, Lord Randolph Churchill, Miss Burke." (1880)

NATIONAL AID LADIES: " A number of ladies have formed themselves into a Committee to alleviate the lot of our brave fellows in Egypt and the Soudan. The Central Committee is composed of the following : (1) Duchess of Marlborough, (2) Mrs. W. Wilton, (3) Miss Higgins, (4) Duchess of Buccleuch, (5) Miss Morck, (6) Countess of Morley, (7) Hon. Lady Lloyd-Lindsay, (8) Lady Louisa Egerton, (9) Countess Brownlow, (10) The Princess of Wales (President), (11) Marchioness of Salisbury, (12) Countess of Rosebery, and (13) Miss Lucy Cohen " (1885)

"SEASIDE EVANGELISM: Our sketch portrays a woman preacher of the gospel striving to sow good seeds among holiday makers. The sound of singing, amid the surf's clashing, is peculiarly melodious, and reminds one of the services of those fishermen of old who knew no vaulted cathedral but that of Heaven, and no altar but the shingle of the Sea of Galilee" (1874)

"ROYAL MUSICIANS: The Princess of Wales and her daughters graciously gave a concert at Brompton Hospital. Their skill afforded great gratification. The Princess played duets with Miss Knollys and the Hon. Mrs. North-Dalrymple, and kindly accompanied various songs" (1888)

" A FLOWER SERVICE IN MAYFAIR : The Princess of Wales and the three young Princesses Louise, Victoria and Maud, attended a Special Floral Service in Berkeley Chapel, which was filled to overflowing by a large juvenile congregation, each member of which presented a bouquet of flowers at the altar rails, until the whole chancel was covered with rare and beautiful blossoms " (1879)

" RECEIVING DAY FOR FOUNDLINGS : Nowadays regulations for the admission of babies to the Foundling Hospital in Guilford Street are very strict. The mothers, assisted by a female attendant, undress their babes and wrap each one in a large grey woollen shawl. The doctor present examines them, after which they are clothed in the garments provided. The doctor presses a bell, three Foundling girls enter, and almost before the mothers are aware, their babies are carried away, never to be known to them again " (1883)

" A GRAND FANCY BAZAAR : This function in aid of the Royal National Hospital for Diseases of the Chest, held at the Duke of Wellington's Riding School, has resulted in a profit of £1,300. Great credit is due to the noble-hearted ladies presiding over the stalls, including the Countess De La Warr, Marchioness of Abergavenny, Countess of Scarborough, Lady Constance Howard, Countess Batthyany, Mrs. Baillie Cochrane, Mrs. Molesworth, Lady Forbes of Newe, Mrs. Arthur D. Sassoon and Mrs. Langtry." (1879)

"GIFTS OF WASTE FISH: A period arrives to every piece of fruit, fish, flesh, and vegetable when it becomes practically unsaleable; and, on the principle of the 'ill wind,' this fact is an agreeable one for very poor people in the West End. Shopkeepers prefer to make a virtue of a necessity, and distribute their waste goods to their destitute neighbours" 1882

"WORMWOOD SCRUBS LECTURES: The Prison Commission having advocated lectures, a start was made at Wormwood Scrubs on 20 'Star' women. Simple phrases were written on the blackboard, for most could read a little. The bandaging became almost professional" 1899)

VII

"STEEL-BOUND AND WHALEBONE-LINED"

CONSIDERED from century to century, costume appears to move in sweeping lines from one phase to another. Considered more closely, from year to year, from season to season, costume degenerates into fashion, which is a thing of rapid ebb and flow, of concentration on minute detail. To describe its almost weekly fluctuations as illustrated in a fashion journal would be wearisome. Only the major changes which took place between the 'sixties and the end of the century will, therefore, find a place in this book.

Save for a brief three years (1878–1880), the fashions followed by our mothers in the heyday of their youth were hideous. The year 1870 marks the change from the graceful if unpractical crinoline to the unpractical but ugly bustle. (It is worth note that the crinoline and the bustle were taken so much for granted that fashion writers of the period never refer to their presence or their gradually changing form.) The crinoline was at its most elegant in the early 'sixties : when the wearer stood still, it made an almost perfect circle round her feet. Above it rose a body made more slender by contrast with the ballooning skirt ; and a small head crowned with a poke bonnet, modified to prettiness, from which depended a little flounce to cover the back hair, and wide ribbons tied in a great bow under the chin. Sophisticated simplicity was the keynote of the hour.

As the 'seventies approached, the crinoline developed a tendency to flatness in the front and distension at the back which, by 1870, had definitely evolved into the bustle. Skirts just swept the ground for promenade wear, were " two fingers " longer for indoor dresses, and for evening trailed a yard or two behind the wearer. By 1873, the stylish wore a bustle extending two feet behind ; 1875 saw a moderating influence, and 1878 witnessed its complete disappearance.

For a few years women were permitted to wear their figures more or less as nature made them : the fashionable mode consisted in a simply cut, close-fitting bodice coming well down the thighs, where it joined a highly elaborate skirt. A normal sized waist was allotted its natural place ; above it was a comely bosom, and below, womanly hips. The difficulty about the charmingly simple, almost tailored upper parts of this period, which were known by such names as the " cuirass " and the " casaquin " bodice, was to keep them as smooth fitting as fashion required. Careful corseting was resorted to ; and fastening manufacturers made frantic efforts to produce a hook-and-eye which would hold the material taut and firm. But with all her efforts no woman who could not abandon her dresses after wearing them half-a-dozen times could manage to present to the world the unwrinkled lines reflected in fashion's mirror.

Below these sternly simple bodices, the skirt broke out into draping, bunching, and folding, with complicated adornments of jet, braid, fringe or lace. The so-called demi-train of dresses designed for morning wear stretched half a yard along the ground—it was, presumably, regarded as the lesser half of the yard-and-a-quarter of richly ornamented material which followed a lady's progress at evening functions.

During this period of simplified figures, that curious garment the dolman enjoyed a vogue. This type of coat was cut in the customary way in front, but had the back and the wide sleeves made in one. At first used for hip length coats only, it gradually grew to three quarter length, and passed imperceptibly into a long, spare cloak fitted closely over the shoulders. It suffered a brief re-birth in 1883 under the new name of the " visite."

A few years of moderate simplicity, and the bustle crept in again. It was her-alded by more and more voluminous bunchings, bows, and foldings below the fitting bodice, and made its re-appearance in the form of a contraption known as the " crinolette," which set the skirt out from the body below the buttocks instead of from the waist.

It is a disillusioning reflection upon the common sense of women that, having permitted themselves to be disembarrassed of such a monstrosity as the bustle, they should have allowed it to be foisted on them afresh. Was it a manufac-turers' conspiracy ?—it is undeniable that its disappearance meant death to an industry in steel and whalebone which had battened on feminine vanity for more than twenty years.

With the return of the bustle began that long period, lasting well into the present century, of self imposed physical torture, due to the fashionable decree that waists were to be small. In the mid-'eighties there is, indeed, a distinctly Elizabethan suggestion about the stylish figure—the bustle behind, growing more and more like the camel's hump in its apparent detachment from the anatomy under it, and a hint of the farthingale at the sides ; with close-fitting bodices coming down into a centre point just below the tiny waist.

That a woman should be prepared to suffer in order to be beautiful is not in-comprehensible ; but that she should put up with semi-strangulation of her vital organs in order to be fashionable would be past belief were it not demon-strable in the history of more than one century (and even in pre-history : witness the wasp waists of the Minoan period). To attain their seventeen-inch waists, the young ladies of the 'eighties and 'nineties submitted to a process of corseting so severe that it required the assistance of another hand, stronger and more re-lentless than their own, to pull the laces tight enough. Their fond mammas felt no shame in giving this assistance. The more sensible, or perhaps one should say the least senseless, submitted to their strait jackets only when abroad, and sought relief in relaxed ·corset strings as soon as they re-entered their homes. But many young women did irreparable harm to their health. Their ill-used ribs were forced inwards on to the liver, with the result that girls fell victims in their hundreds to the " green sickness," the common name for chlorosis, a form of anæmia among young women which has nearly disappeared from the medico's case list. Yet all the time purveyors of corsets were advertising their wares as admirable inventions, medically perfect, and giving " support " where

" MANTLES FROM PARIS : (1) Bonnet of black velvet trimmed with lace. Mantle of black velvet richly embroidered in silk and ornamented with a row of broad black guipure and pleated headings made of black sarsnet ribbon. The dress is of bright blue silk, trimmed with velvet. (2) Bonnet of black velvet, with a roll of black and magenta velvet in front, and black feathers tipped with magenta behind. The circular mantle is of thick corded silk, with straps of velvet edged with narrow Maltese lace, and pointed rows of narrow jet trimming. (3) Black velvet bonnet trimmed with flat bows of green ribbon.

Mantle of dark grey cloth, scalloped at the bottom. Over the shoulders a black silk scalloped pelerine. Pale green broché silk dress, figured with black. (4) Bonnet of black silk and white terry velvet, trimmed with white roses and black and white feathers. The pardessus of black velvet is made tightly fitting to the figure. Black guipure is inserted on each side in a bell shape, finished off with rows of jet trimming. (5) Drab velvet bonnet trimmed with scarlet ribbon and a quilling of black lace. Cloth mantle trimmed with a silk braid, the sleeves and back being cut in one piece. The dress is of poplin" (1861)

"FOR THE AFTERNOON : A Striped Foulard Skirt, plaited into a Swiss band corded with black silk, to correspond with the stripe on the foulard. A high White Muslin Bodice, formed with puffings separated with strips of insertion embroidered in satin stitch. A narrow Valenciennes lace around the throat and wrists. This toilette is suitable for a young lady. For a married lady is a Checked Foulard Dress, the skirt ornamented with three narrow plaited flounces ; a Mantle Scarf trimmed with the same. A White Horsehair Bonnet, trimmed with blue and black taffetas, the blue plaiting at the top being fastened down in the centre with a strap of horsehair and buttons made of black, blue, and white silk. The child is wearing a White Alpaca Frock, ornamented with a strap of the same, with blue velvet buttons down the centre. There are buttons upon the short sleeves, and the bodice is bordered round the top with black velvet. The Boots are blue satin jean " (1863)

support is required ! More significant is the stress laid on their strength, which is said to have been such that they would not break under the greatest strain.

The year 1889 brought a diminished bustle and a hint of the leg-o'-mutton sleeve—the aberration which was to dominate the fashions of the 'nineties. In the course of 1890, the bustle faded into oblivion—let us hope for all time—and the leg-o'-mutton sleeve established itself firmly. The next two years brought longer waists, more constricted ribs, and higher chests. The pouter pigeon figure, induced by raised bosom, flattened stomach, and pronounced posterior, was the favoured line of 1893, when frills, enormous revers, capes and capelets added to puffed sleeves made a woman twice as broad across the shoulders as across the hips. Shrunken sleeves standing up increasingly above the shoulder ; tight floor length skirts ; and bonnets with aigrettes gave the dull fashions of 1894 their one touch of distinction—excessive stiffness and an effect of immense height.

The leg-o'-mutton sleeve, swelling and shrinking by turns, reached its zenith in 1895, when women wore immense sleeves, each one puffed out wider than the body. In that year skirts began to sweep the floor again, and throats were encased in tall, tight collars. This style underwent gradual modification until it finally merged into the Gibson girl figure of the end of the century—deep bosomed, full bottomed, with a tinier waist than ever before, a flowing skirt, pouched bodice, and a slight leg-o'-mutton sleeve slowly fading into a long, close-fitting one.

Never since the Middle Ages, when people dressed not merely themselves but their beds in funereal black, had mourning been so emphatic as it was in the 'seventies. It remained in force, a slowly relenting, but still painstakingly regulated system, until the Great War made mourning so universal that its outward showing became superfluous. The widowed Queen, who wore mourning weeds for her Prince during a quarter of a century—until, indeed, she slightly relaxed her garb for her Jubilee in 1887—set the tone in this phase of fashion. With a grim familial tenacity she remembered her multitudinous relations to the nth degree, and the Court was continually being plunged into mourning on the death of some remotely related German royalty of whose life this country had known nothing.

Manuals on the " Etiquette of Mourning " were published, and every dressmaker, milliner, and draper's assistant was versed in the correct scale of lamentation by trimming which it was the duty of the seemly widow and orphan to assume. One of the big London shops advertised regularly that, " on receipt of letter or telegram," they would forward " mourning goods to all parts of England on approbation—no matter the distance—with an excellent-fitting Dressmaker (if required), without extra charge." In view of the size of the Victorian home circle, and the fact that servants as well as members of the family were tricked out in the customary suits of solemn black, the resulting

orders must have been well worth the expense involved in the despatch of that
" excellent-fitting Dressmaker."

Mourning had one decidedly bright aspect : in the days when durability was
the first quality demanded of a material, a death was the only occasion on which
the younger and smaller children could hope for new clothes. At other times
they had to make do with frocks and suits discarded by their elder sisters and
brothers in rotation. One typical advertisement of serge asserts that in its second
winter, mother can make it over into another dress for herself " as good as
new," in its third year it can be cut down for her daughter, in its fourth made
into a suit for her small son, after which the charwoman's little boy can still get
another year or two's wear out of it. . . . And in her book of memories, *Life's
Ebb and Flow*, the Countess of Warwick describes how, heiress as she was,
" to my deep chagrin, until I was sixteen or so, my dresses were made out of my
mother's cast-off gowns." Yet she was allowed £2,000 for the purchase of her
wedding trousseau.

Hair and head coverings were at least as variable as the dress of the period.
The small flounced poke bonnets of 1861 were as far from the flat bonnets of
1868, tied under the chin or dangling streamers behind to the shoulders, as the
tip tilted hats of 1870, worn over the left eye and adorned with ostrich tips,
flowers, and long fringed scarves, were from the straight-set hats and bonnets of
1889, with their upstanding bows, feathers, and birds, or the plain sailor hat of
the 'nineties which was the correct wear for sporting occasions. The curls of
the eighteen-sixties lingered on into the 'seventies ; but about 1870 it was more
fashionable to have the back of the head and nape of the neck draped in heavy
plaits. By 1875 the hair was dressed high, in a coronet of wreathed braids, and
hats, loaded with birds and velvet bows, perched perilously on top, threatening
momently to slide off backwards. By 1885 less hair was worn : a single big curl
rolled on top of the head sufficed fashion's demands.

A bun twisted up on the crown held sway throughout the 'nineties. During
the earlier years of the decade, the hair was arranged close to the head ; by 1899
it was worn much fluffed out—a fashion for those with naturally wavy hair, not
for the straight haired, whose efforts at achieving the elegant head were usually
marred by stray ends round the back of the neck.

Baldness was a not uncommon complaint among women ; advertisements for
its cure are frequent. And most ladies added something to their own natural
growth—a swathe, a fringe, a toupet, or a few pin-curls. These might equally
well have grown on someone else's head or be the prudent garnerings of their
own hair tidies, which in 1877 could be prepared and made up at 3*s.* 6*d.* an
ounce : a reasonable price, considering how many hairs go to the ounce.

It must not be supposed that every woman sheepishly followed the dictates of
later Victorian fashion. There were spasmodic revolts, and, undermining the
whole crazy structure, the changing mode of life of the average woman. Young
girls, under the influence of Morris, signed pledges not to wear the crinolette,

" PARISIAN FASHIONS : On the left, a foulard dress with a *ruche* above the hem. A small casaque trimmed with a *ruche* upon the edge, epaulettes, and sleeves. A pink tulle bonnet ; a wreath formed with black ribbons ; similar ribbons falling in plaits at the back. On the right, a grey linos dress over a petticoat of the same material. The skirt is looped up with gimp bands, and trimmed with narrow black ribbon velvet. The paletôt is ornamented to correspond. The hat is bordered with black velvet, and trimmed with a feather, a rose, and white tulle lappets. *Gants de Suèdes* with three buttons are in order, as are light kid boots " (1865)

"FULL EVENING DRESS : Robe consisting of under-skirt of white silk, trimmed to form a petticoat in front, with two inch folds of black silk headed at a short distance by a narrower one ; a plaiting of white stands up from the narrow fold forming three rows of trimming ; a scollop of silk laid on the underskirt to form a train ; there are several rows of plaiting above, some standing up, and one coming down in the direction of the scollop ; a trimming of black cord is put on the scollop, and a similar cord divides the plaiting. Over-train and tunic of black silk, with the tunic taken up each side in ample folds, falling deep down the front of the dress ; it is secured each side with a gore of the underskirt brought outside and carried to waist ; a deep fringe borders the tunic and sides of train, and the back of the train, which is very long, is decorated with three bands ". (1870)

and associations were started in the 'seventies, both in England and abroad, with the object of simplifying dress. One such " band of sedate Englishwomen " pledged themselves to " a convenient livery of perpetual black." The æsthetic movement of the early 'eighties, guyed by W. S. Gilbert in *Patience*, was, in spite of its fatuous artiness, a genuine protest against the absurdities of contemporary dress.

The divided skirt, christened " bloomers " after its most ardent advocate, Mrs. Amelia Jenks Bloomer, was an American product of the late 'forties. It was resuscitated in 1882 without much success by Lady Harberton, who pressed its claims at an exhibition of " Hygienic Wearing Apparel " ; and it had quite a vogue in the 'nineties, when the arrival of the safety bicycle made it imperatively necessary that women should wear a garment more suitable to their new exercise than the skirt of the day.

Women's increasing open-air activities—tennis, golf, rowing, mountaineering, as well as the supremely important cycling—brought inevitably a semblance of utility into some even of the fashionable clothes designed in the 'nineties. The sportswoman's " tailor-mades " and the modes for wet weather, though both heavy and voluminous, were yet distinctly simpler and more convenient than the " practical promenade toilettes " intended for saunters in the Park.

Underwear between 1870 and 1900 showed a notable advance in simplicity. Unæsthetic as the combinations of the 'nineties were, they were an improvement hygienically and as labour savers both on the ample, frilled, lace burdened chemises and sweeping, flounced petticoats of the 'seventies, and on the quilted petticoats and elaborate " tournures " of the 'eighties. The dread of the human body which haunted the Victorian mind was responsible for the efforts made by fashion to obscure as well as to cover the lines of that fearful monster, the flesh. The Brownings, ardent lovers as they were, never saw one another naked ; and the same must be true of most Victorian couples. This attitude of mind is reflected even more crudely in the swathings of the nightgowns and underwear worn in the 'seventies, and the aggressive plainness of the combinations which came in during the 'nineties, than in the often superficially elegant concealments of the outer covering. Until the late 'eighties, ladies were never shown inside the underwear which figures in the pattern sections and advertisement pages of weekly papers.

I owe sincere thanks to the Proprietors of the *Queen* newspaper for their courtesy in allowing me access to their files and for permitting the reproduction of the pictures in this chapter. While these do not attempt to give a complete survey of fashion during the last forty years of Queen Victoria's reign, they do indicate its vagaries at a period when its charm was closely akin to ugliness.

"MORNING TOILETTES: The toilette on the left is suitable to a young girl from fourteen to sixteen years of age. It consists of a short skirt trimmed with narrow velvet and buttons, and covered with a black silk tunic, which forms also a corselet, and is cut out in festoons round the edge; it crosses at the side like a *polonaise*. The bodice is made of the same material as the skirt, but the epaulettes are velvet. Small Valenciennes necktie, with coral brooch. The second toilette is of black alpaca. The first skirt is trimmed with three narrow crossbands of satin; the second skirt, which is ornamented in the same style, is looped up first on each side, with a bow without ends, and at the back it forms a *pouf*, which is kept in its place by the bow of the sash. The high bodice is trimmed round the armholes, throat, and cuffs with crossbands of satin. Bows on the shoulder, and a plaiting at the back above the waistband, both likewise of satin " (1868)

" WIDOW'S FIRST MOURNING : This dress is made of a peculiar silk called ' radz de mort ' expressly manufactured in Spital-fields for this class of mourning. It is trimmed with quadruple crape, which is proof against ruffling or discolourment by heat or rain. This crape is both durable and dressy " (1872)

" DEEP MOURNING : Woollen armure trimmed with crape, the skirt bordered with three crosscut tucks of crape, the tunic trimmed with crossbands. The tablier, round in front, square at the back, is draped with two series of gathers. Joan of Arc bodice, cuffs and plaiting at throat of crape " (1875)

"AUTUMN ROBE DE CHAMBRE: Princesse robe of vicuna cloth, with astra-chan trimmings and old silver buttons. It fastens with a flap ornamented with an astrachan border." (Left) "FOR A GIRL OF TEN: White piqué jacket trimmed with white muslin plaitings, grey mohair frock piped with blue. The skirt is bordered with a deep flounce, and the tablier is trimmed with three narrower ones. Two flounces form a festooned tunic at the back of the skirt, and are looped up with blue bows." (Top left) "GIRL'S POLONAISE: This polonaise is in the new style with a long waistcoat. It looks more stylish if waistcoat and cuffs are in a contrasting colour. The binding at the edge of the revers must match the waistcoat" (1873)

"LA VALLIERE": trimmed with myrtle-green China crape, an aigrette of flowers, and a brilliant humming bird (1873)

" BROWN FELT BONNET, with velvet flowers and leaves, and a basket-woven ribbon terminating in a bow " (1875)

" BLACK STRAW HAT, trimmed with black velvet, black feathers, a green bird, and the new Merveilleux satin " (1879)

" BERET TOQUE of dark blue velvet ornamented with dark blue and yellow pompoms on the black silk brim " (1880)

" THE ALEXANDRA TOURNURE : This style of tournure or bustle has now taken the place of crinoline under costumes. It gives that fulness at the back of the skirt below the waist which fashion now decrees. The materials required are brillanté and narrow steels, cord and elastic. For winter wear flannel might be substituted for the white brillanté " (1872)

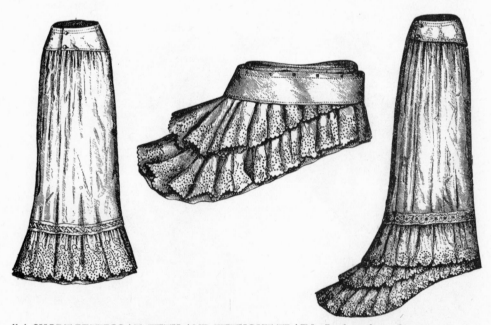

" A SHORT PETTICOAT, WITH AND WITHOUT TRAIN : In these days of moving about a petticoat that can be worn under both a short and a long dress is a convenience. Our illustrations clearly show this most useful contrivance. There is (1) the short petticoat, (2) the loose train, and (3) the train buttoned on. The materials are cambric and English embroidery " (1880)

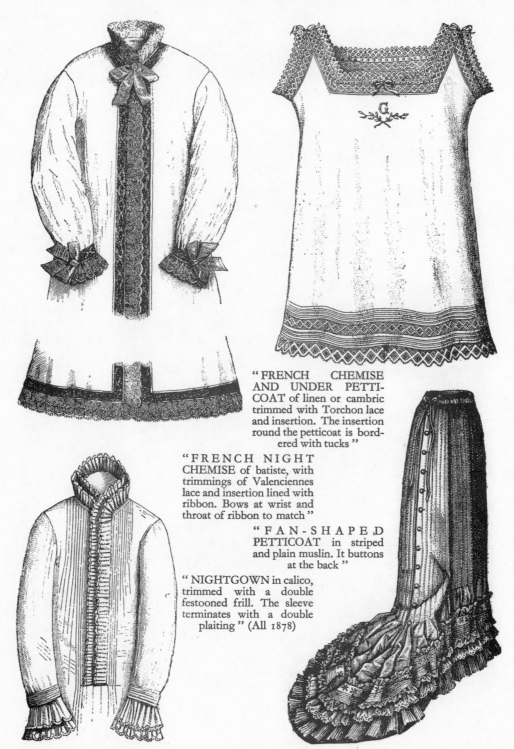

" FRENCH CHEMISE AND UNDER PETTI-COAT of linen or cambric trimmed with Torchon lace and insertion. The insertion round the petticoat is bordered with tucks "

" FRENCH NIGHT CHEMISE of batiste, with trimmings of Valenciennes lace and insertion lined with ribbon. Bows at wrist and throat of ribbon to match "

" FAN-SHAPED PETTICOAT in striped and plain muslin. It buttons at the back "

" NIGHTGOWN in calico, trimmed with a double festooned frill. The sleeve terminates with a double plaiting " (All 1878)

"LATEST PARIS FASHIONS: (1) Afternoon dress in checked brown and grey bége and brown faille. The skirt bordered with a faille flounce, headed with checked bouillonné. Princess tunic ornamented, like the sleeves and bodice, with crossbands of faille; (2) Carriage dress in blue faille and blue checked velvet trimmed with borders of natural feathers; (3) Promenade costume of dark green faille and green and yellow woollen. Tunic square at one side, round at the other, edged with braid and fringe. Cuirass bodice; (4) Carriage dress of iron-grey Indian cashmere and black velvet trimmed with feather bordering. The bodice terminates in front with long square ends, buttoning the entire length; (5) Morning outdoor costume of black faille and grey and black woollen bége. The tunic ornamented with buttons and a crossband of velvet. Joan of Arc bodice; (6) Indoor costume in prune-coloured Indian cashmere. The skirt bordered with a faille plaiting, headed with six rows of braid. Polonaise with one square basque at the back; the left side is round. A pointed pocket on the basque" (1875)

"STEEL–BOUND AND WHALEBONE–LINED"

"YOUNG LADIES' DEMI TOILETTES: The first consists of an embroidered muslin skirt, falling over a deep flounce of the same; overdress of Indian silk trimmed with velvet of a darker shade; the sash is velvet, also the rosette; the sleeve and plastron match the skirt. Number two is of braided cashmere and satin of a darker shade. The plastron is gathered and crossed with brandeburgs composed of braid and the back of the skirt is draped. Number three, dark green skirt and corselet with embroidered nun's-veiling tunic and bodice. The sash and bow are velvet ribbon. A bouillonné edges the skirt. Number four, fawn cashmere, velvet and soft silk. The guimpe is of the silk, trimmings are ribbon velvet" (1883)

"WASHING COSTUMES: (1) Pompom sateen with nasturtium yellow ground and brown spots. Plastron, belt and sleeve trimmings in Ottoman silk of a darker brown. (2) Pale cream Surah trimmed with imitation Mechlin lace. Satin bow. Tiny slashes on the sleeve. The overdress is looped at the back with bows" (1883)

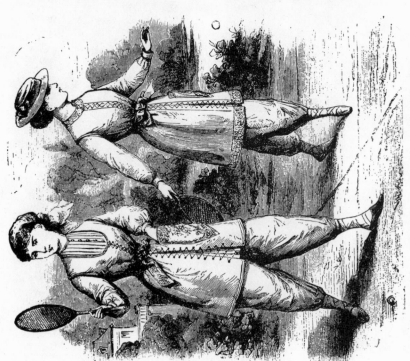

"FOR LAWN-TENNIS: This adaptation of the Moorish costume still worn in Portugal has been adopted by the English colony at Oporto for lawn-tennis. The sleeveless bodice is worn over a shirt with long loose sleeves. The serge skirt is laced. Full and flowing Eastern pantaloons, tightly laced to the ankle, cover the legs" (1880)

" CHILDREN'S OUTDOOR COSTUMES : (1) For a girl of six : The long plain serge bodice has a striped full skirt attached. The plastron and lower part of the sleeves are striped. (2) The Moujik costume : Bronze serge blouse, trimmed with striped velvet of the same shade. (3) For a girl of ten : Costume for fêtes in green plush and rich guipure. The bodice opens over a guipure plastron. The guipure revers form a round collar at the back ; mousquetaire cuffs. (4) For a girl of five : Cream cashmere embroidered in red. The scarf is fastened with a velvet bow, an embroidered flounce forms a second skirt. (5) For a girl of four : An over-dress in canvas trimmed with écru embroidery. Bows on the shoulders. (6) Front of the Moujik costume. (7) Front of (1) " (1885)

"WEDDING GROUP: This illustration shows the manner in which pages carry the bride's train, and the youngest bridesmaids throw flowers in her path. The bride's dress is of ivory satin trimmed with lace and orange blossom. The sleeves are entirely of lace and so is the upper part of the bodice, the lace being worked with pearls. The pages wear dark blue plush suits, lined with gold satin, and the bridesmaids white veiling with blue moiré sashes and lace collars. Their stockings are blue silk and they carry gilt baskets in their hands. The bride carries a mass of white lilac tied with long streamers of white velvet ribbon" (1885)

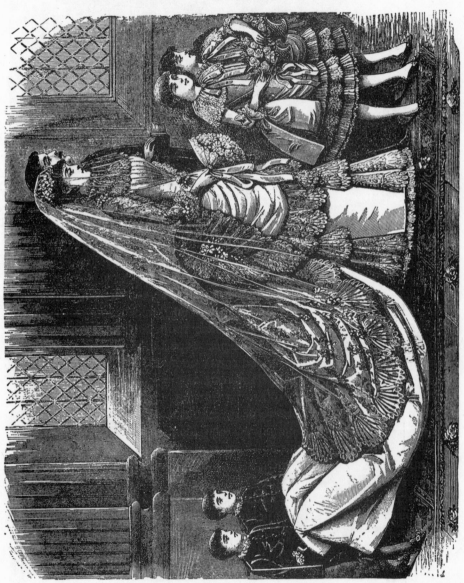

" TAILOR JACKETS FOR SPRING WEAR. (1) Stone coloured diagonal cloth, secured below the waist with a clasp of gilt buttons. Coat facings in steel grey velvet ; full front in cream flannel, and demi-belt in grey pongee silk. (2) African brown tweed relieved with straight facings, covered with an embroidery in gold and black cord. (3) Close fitting vest in red blotting-paper ladies' cloth, plainly trimmed with rows of stitching and braid sewn over the seams. (4) Tomato red elastic cloth, ornamented with black moiré cuffs and facings. It opens slightly at the throat to display the collar of the under dress. (5) Jacket of tan coloured summer cloth, embellished with gold braiding on revers and cuffs" (1889)

(Left) "THE BOULOGNE VISITE: Dark red cloth trimmed with rows of narrow metallic braid, and buttons to correspond. The visite fits the figure at the back, where it is plaited, and has dolman sleeves. The braid is sown (sic) on the right front of the jacket to simulate revers". (1885)

(Right) "THE JERSEY JACKET: Dark chocolate brown corduroy, lined with old gold satin, and furnished with side pockets. The jacket is close fitting at the back, and somewhat loose at the front. It is fastened with painted mussel-shell buttons, with a similar button on each sleeve". (1885)

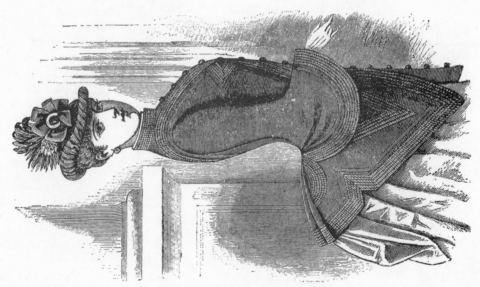

" FOR YACHTING AND BOATING : (1) Gown of navy blue serge and blue and white spotted foulard, ornamented with gold and silver braid. Hat of navy blue straw. (2) Gown of navy blue serge with vest, underskirt and half-sleeves of red cloth, braided in navy blue and gold ; Medici collar and revers in red. Hat of white straw with red brim. (3) Costume of blue serge combined with blue and white striped serge. Hat of navy blue straw. (4) Gown of cream foulé serge braided in double gold cord. Fringed sash at the side " (1890)

" SEASIDE AND BATHING COSTUMES : (1) Brown serge bathing dress embellished with bands, rays, and fringed sash in écru ; (2) Child's bathing costume in white bunting, enlivened with red braid ; (3) Bathing costume, with draped braces and pleated skirt, in terra cotta Devonshire serge trimmed with white braid ; (4) Costume with draped bodice in bois de rose cotton finely striped with almond green ; puffed epaulettes, and accordion pleated skirt ; chemisette and cuffs in plain bois de rose cotton, striped with white. Rows of washing galon encircle the skirt. Swiss belt in green moiré silk ; (5) Costume in white sateen powdered with green design, with which harmonise the ribbons, straps, and bows ; ornamented with guipure work ; (6) Child's dress in cream tennis flannel, trimmed with braid ; (7) Child's frock in peach coloured alpaca, smartened up with loops of washing ribbon ; scarf in soft serge silk " (1889)

" RIDING HABITS AND CYCLING GOWN : (1) Habit in Moleton cloth, pointed bodice opening V-shape to display a shirt front with stud and necktie complete ; (2) Jacket and skirt in grey or blue tweed or serge, ornamented with a few rows of either machine stitching or braid ; blouse bodice in thin white flannel, tucked in in front ; cloth gaiters and peaked cap to correspond, the latter being decorated in front with a club device or tricycle ; (3) Riding habit in black ladies' cloth, close fitting bodice buttoned in front, and leaving but a small opening to show off the flat tie in either cambric or washing silk " (1889)

"FOR THE RACES: (1) Corselet, Zouave jacket, and skirt in plum-coloured velvet trimmed with gold galon. High sleeves, puckered and fastened with buttons in amethyst crystal, kerchief, and overskirt in Ophelia-coloured China silk. Auriole hat in white aerophane with a plum-coloured velvet torsade; (2) Princess robe in écru beige canvas. Ornamented across the seamless bodice and on the skirt with turquoise embroidery sparkling with crystal beads. Sleeves, neckband, and flutings of skirt of blue pongee silk. Hat in fancy white straw, enhanced with bows of white muslin, blue Ottoman ribbon, and tinsel gauze; (3) Coat in Louis XVI brocade opening to display an underskirt of white China crape, embellished with multi-coloured embroidery. Crownless toque ornamented with wild oats; (4) Gown in pearl grey de laine. Jockey sleeves in keeping. Demi-bodice, long sleeves, and front panel in pink figured de laine. Velvet throatlet in Eiffel red brown. Picturesque hat in Tuscan straw with white and pink ostrich feathers " (1800)

" FASHIONABLE FURS : This handsome coat in finest Alaska sealskin, cut semi-fitting and trimmed with the richest Russian Sable, is the latest style for winter wear " (1893)

" TEA GOWN, by Worth, in soft woollen material shaded from creamy white to dark chestnut brown ; the lightest tint represents the bodice, while the deepest reaches to the edges of the three-cornered train. The long sleeves have ruchings in white batiste divided into puffings with bands of guipure, also used on bodice and jacket " (1893)

" A STYLISH TAILOR-MADE : This dark blue serge skirt with smart little short jacket is the perfection of neatness, with its rolled back collar faced with white cloth and belt fastened with a gold buckle. It is worn with a tailored blouse and one of the fashionable boaters, and has been made for the trousseau of the Princess Maud of Wales " (1896)

" STEEL–BOUND AND WHALEBONE–LINED "

(Left) " YOUNG LADY'S HAT : Turquoise blue scalloped straw, wreathed with forget-me-not blue ostrich feathers, and connected together in the centre with a rosette bow in mauve silk, displaying a paste buckle ; white willowy aigrette springing out from another rosette on the crown" (1898)

(Right) " HAT IN FANCY STRAW : Emerald-green and silver-grey mixture, relieved with variegated roses. A long black ostrich feather covers the crown, a smaller one stands up as a plume colonel " (1898)

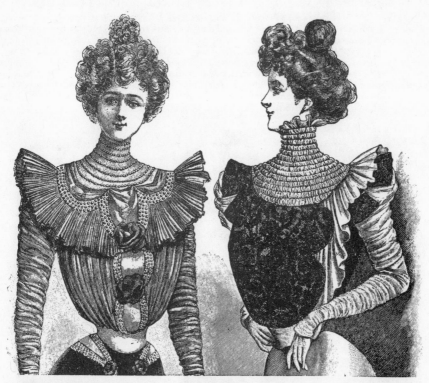

" THEATRE BLOUSES : (1) Pink silk muslin, with pearl encircled transparent yoke and neck-band united to a shoulder frill in finely pleated muslin by a festooned band of mirror velvet, sprinkled with cut crystal cabochons. Stomacher and hip-band in keeping. Choux in black lisse. (2) Closely gaged yoke, rucked sleeves. Neck ruffle and brace-like frill in cream silk muslin. Low blouse and battlemented epaulettes of black jetted guipure over ruby satin " (1898)

CORSETS : (1) " Dr. Wardrop's Cuirass corset has attached under it a light strong plate which gives the stomach a flatness and grace even if inclined to embonpoint. The medical profession strongly recommend this corset after accouchement, as the figure is entirely remodelled without undue pressure " (1883) ; (2) " With Adjustable Belt : the object of combining Corset and Belt is to entirely avoid the discomforts which a separate Belt causes by continually getting displaced and not affording the necessary support. Strongly recommended by doctors " (1893) ; (3) " The Spécialité is manufactured under scientific supervision, the cut and make being perfect ; each bone is placed in the position requiring support, without impeding or checking the proper exercise of the muscles, allowing perfect freedom of action to the whole frame " (1893)

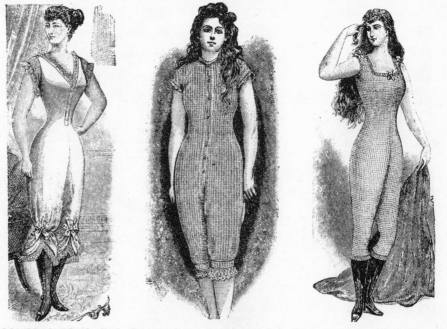

COMBINATIONS : " The Deeanjay " (1893) ; " The Cellular " (1892) ; " The Eclipse " (1896)